Hg
Rn
I
U
Sc
B
Po
In
Ar
V
Ge

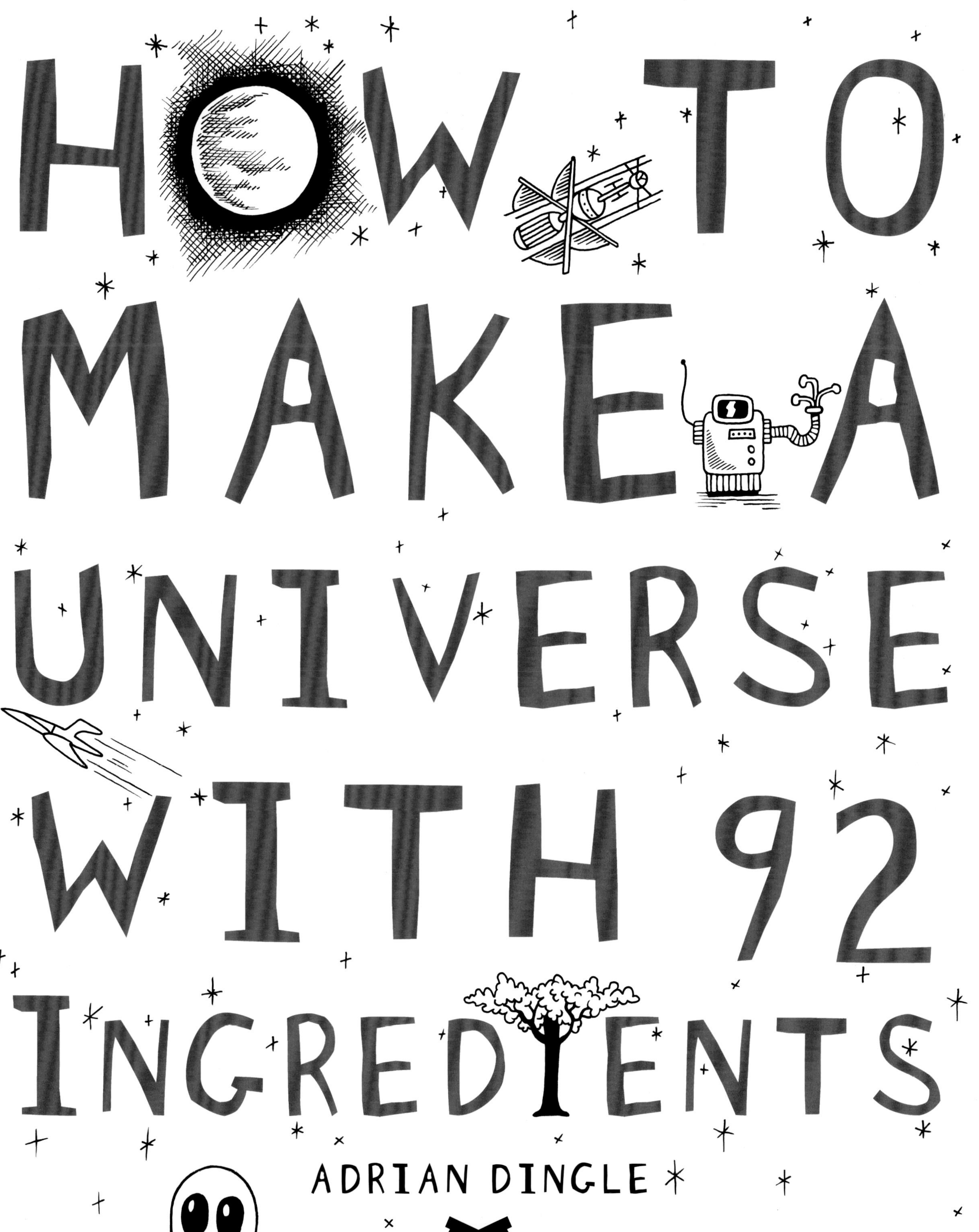

HOW TO MAKE A UNIVERSE WITH 92 INGREDIENTS

ADRIAN DINGLE

Owl kids

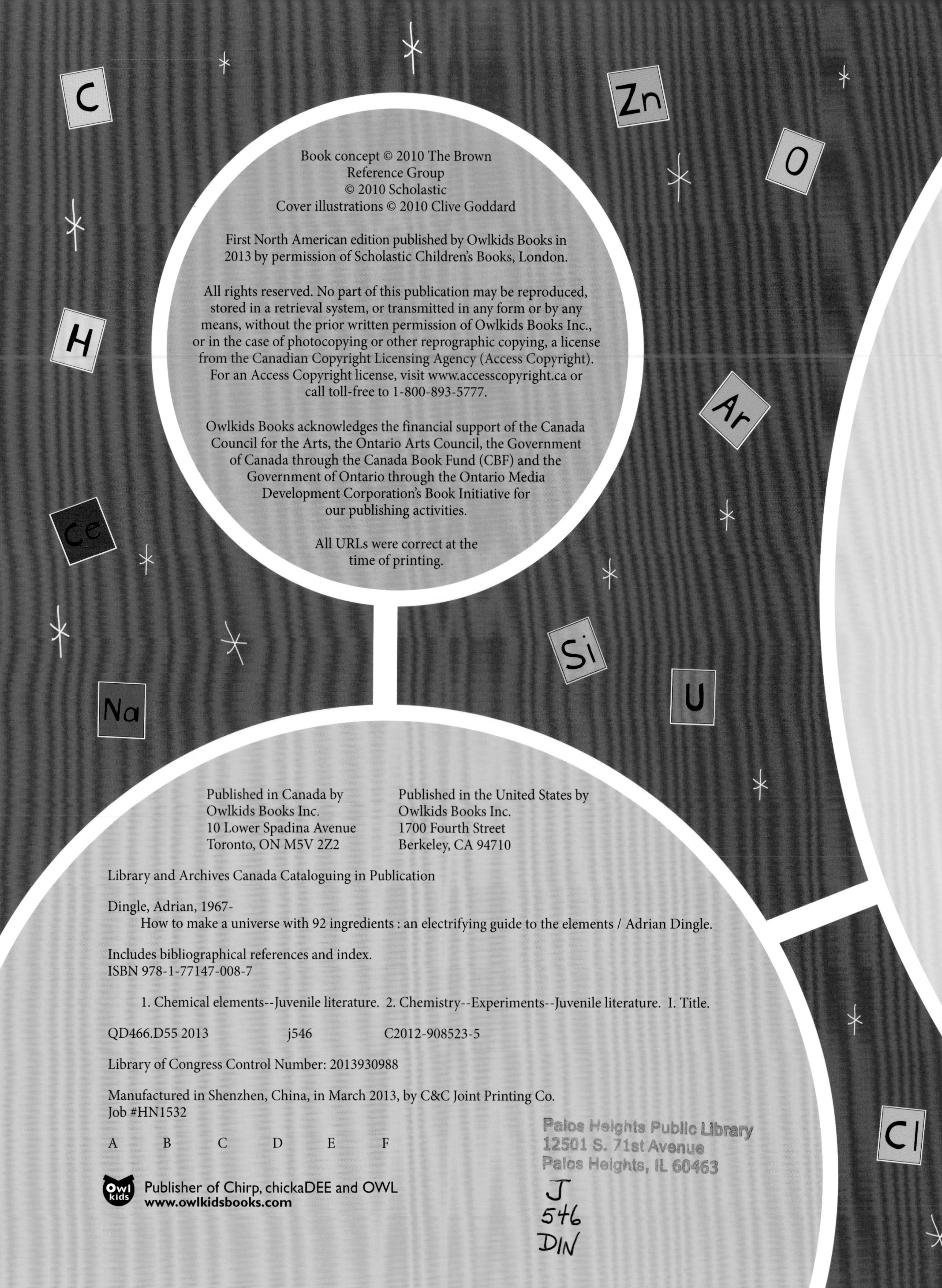

First North American edition published by Owlkids Books in 2013 by permission of Scholastic Children's Books, London.

Owlkids Books acknowledges the financial support of the Canada Council for the Arts, the Ontario Arts Council, the Government of Canada through the Canada Book Fund (CBF) and the Government of Ontario through the Ontario Media Development Corporation's Book Initiative for our publishing activities.

All URLs were correct at the time of printing.

Published in Canada by
Owlkids Books Inc.
10 Lower Spadina Avenue
Toronto, ON M5V 2Z2

Published in the United States by
Owlkids Books Inc.
1700 Fourth Street
Berkeley, CA 94710

Library and Archives Canada Cataloguing in Publication

Dingle, Adrian, 1967-
How to make a universe with 92 ingredients : an electrifying guide to the elements / Adrian Dingle.

Includes bibliographical references and index.
ISBN 978-1-77147-008-7

1. Chemical elements--Juvenile literature. 2. Chemistry--Experiments--Juvenile literature. I. Title.

QD466.D55 2013 j546 C2012-908523-5

Library of Congress Control Number: 2013930988

Manufactured in Shenzhen, China, in March 2013, by C&C Joint Printing Co.
Job #HN1532

A B C D E F

Publisher of Chirp, chickaDEE and OWL
www.owlkidsbooks.com

CONTENTS

H
Cl
Science nerd ALERT!
Zn
Si
What goes on inside an atom?
Br
Al
At
Ti
The PAGES of this book were made with Carbon.
Be
Kr
6
12.01
C
CARBON
1
1.01
H
HYDROGEN
HOW TO MAKE A UNIVERSE WITH 92 INGREDIENTS
WARNING GRIPPING!
Cf
As
Fe

THIS BOOK...

...shows you how ELEMENTS combine to make loads of things (everything, in fact!). The book has four chapters, but they all overlap a bit so you can read them in any order—though it might be best to start with the next few pages. There's a list of chemistry words at the back, if you need any reminders.

IT'S ELEMENTARY

This book is about elements. There aren't many of them, but they make up everything you see. They make up the world. In fact, they make up the whole universe. Oh...and they make up YOU, too!

Chemists define an element as a substance that cannot be broken down into simpler substances by chemical means. In other words, if we take an element and try a chemical reaction with it, it cannot become any LESS complicated. It can only become MORE complicated. For example, it can form a compound, say, by bonding together with a bunch of other elements. Each element is made up of very, very, very tiny particles called atoms. In turn, the atoms are made of subatomic particles: protons, neutrons, and electrons. All of the atoms of a particular element have the same number of protons and electrons. The number of protons DEFINES the element. If the atoms have eight protons, the element is oxygen; if there are nine protons, it's fluorine, and so on. The number of protons is called the atomic number. All the elements are listed in an arrangement called the periodic table in order of atomic number, starting with number 1, hydrogen. Oxygen is number 8.

The protons and neutrons form a dense nucleus, or center; the electrons arrange themselves around the outside.

Scientists try to learn about atoms by SMASHING them together and seeing what smaller bits fly off.

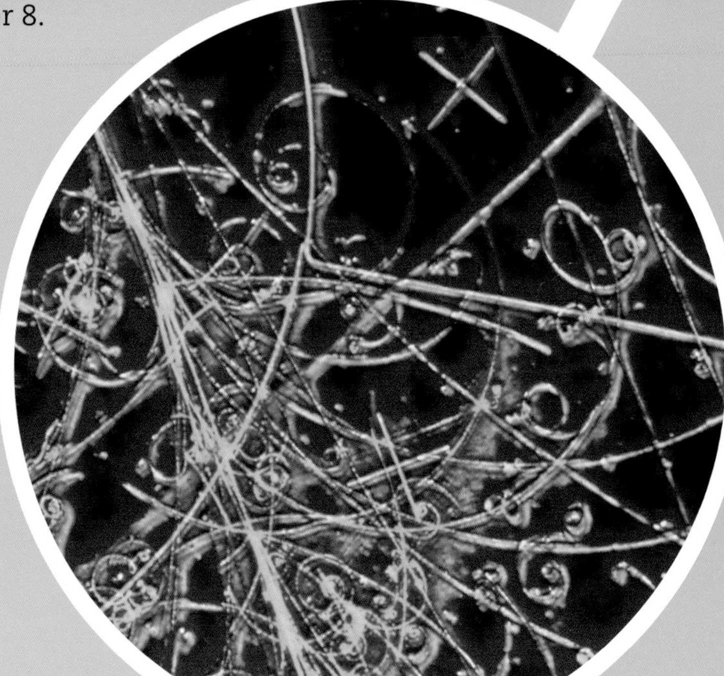

SPIN!

Neutron numbers

Although the atoms of an element have fixed numbers of protons and electrons, they can have different numbers of neutrons. Atoms of the same element with different numbers of neutrons are called isotopes. Most elements have several isotopes. Chlorine, for example, has two common types of atom; both have 17 protons and 17 electrons, but one has 18 neutrons and the other has 20 neutrons. The different numbers of neutrons mean that the different isotopes have different masses.

Are there really 92 naturally occurring elements?

Well, yes...and no. All the elements with atomic numbers 1 to 92 do occur on Earth. But it's a bit more complicated than that! Of the 92 naturally occurring elements, some are very, VERY rare. Francium (87) and astatine (85) make up less than an ounce (no more than a few grams) each in the Earth's crust at any one time. Other radioactive elements from when Earth was formed (over 4.5 BILLION years ago) have virtually disappeared by decaying naturally, like technetium (43) and promethium (61). Elements 93 and 94 (neptunium and plutonium) also occur naturally, but again in ultra-tiny amounts. So, depending on which elements you count, you could argue that there are as few as 88 natural elements on Earth or as many as 94.

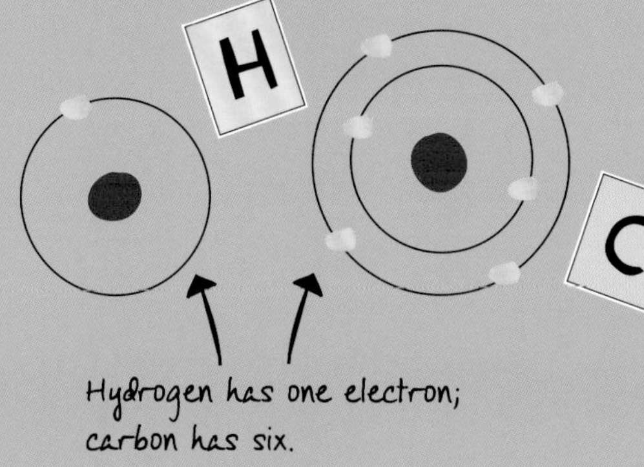

Hydrogen has one electron; carbon has six.

Every element has a symbol that is an abbreviation of its name. Some are pretty crazy, like Pb (lead). They're often based on elements' old names—but they've stuck!

Above number 92

A periodic table (there's one on the next page) lists elements with atomic numbers higher than 92, up into the 100s. These elements don't occur naturally on Earth; they have to be made in laboratories. IUPAC (the International Union of Pure and Applied Chemistry) currently recognizes 112 elements (number 112 doesn't have an official name or symbol yet). These super-heavy elements are all radioactive; in many cases only a few atoms have ever been produced, maybe for only fractions of a second. This usually means that they are not much use BUT at least one of these synthetic elements may be in your house RIGHT NOW! Element number 95, americium, is used widely in smoke detectors!

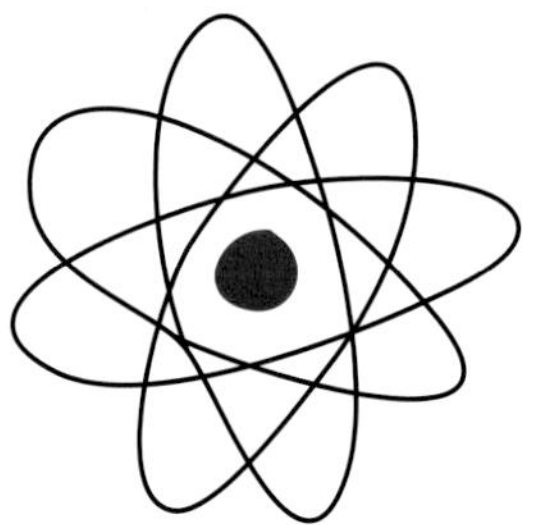

The Periodic TABLE

The periodic table tells us loads about the elements and how they behave. It's like a guide to the whole universe...all on a single piece of paper.

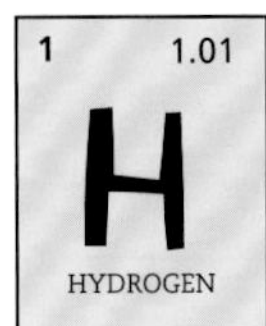

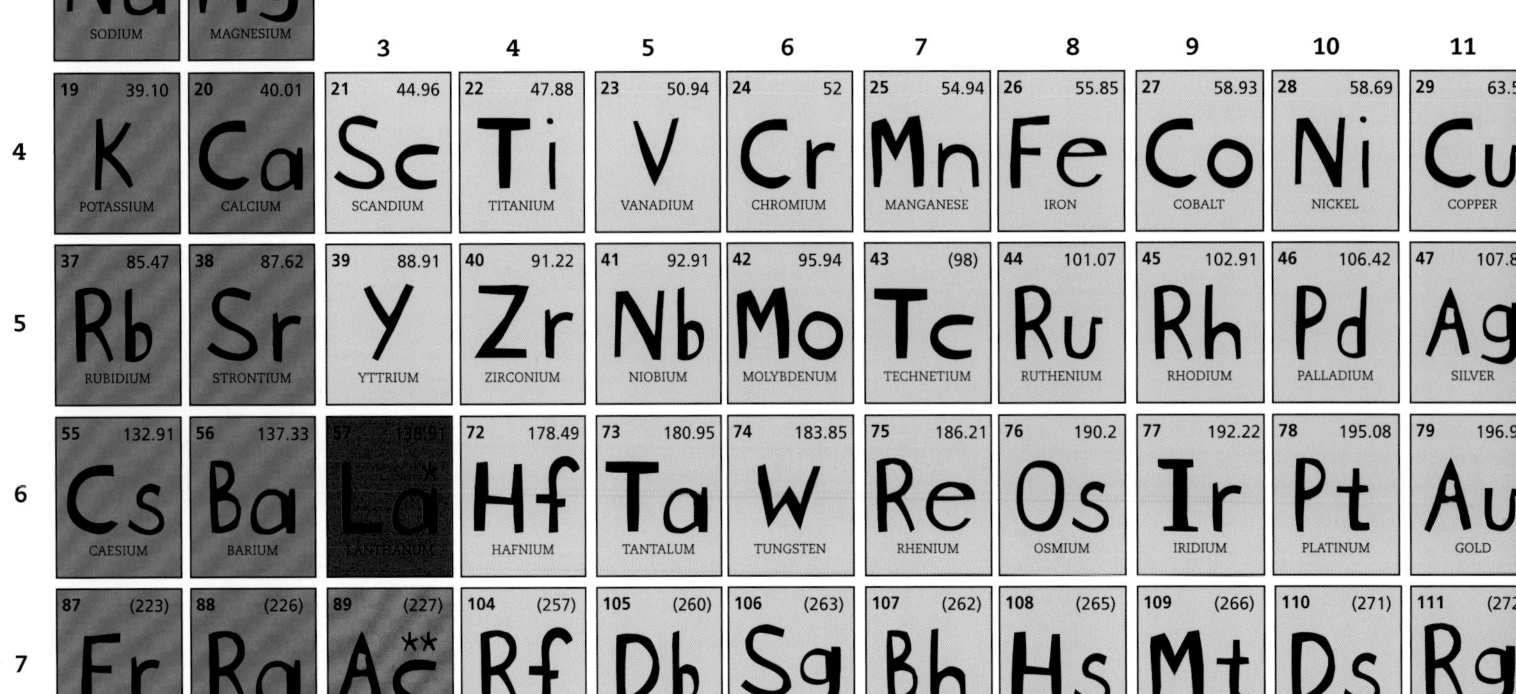

	1	2	3	4	5	6	7	8	9	10	11
1	1 1.01 H HYDROGEN										
2	3 6.94 Li LITHIUM	4 9.01 Be BERYLLIUM									
3	11 23.00 Na SODIUM	12 24.31 Mg MAGNESIUM									
4	19 39.10 K POTASSIUM	20 40.01 Ca CALCIUM	21 44.96 Sc SCANDIUM	22 47.88 Ti TITANIUM	23 50.94 V VANADIUM	24 52 Cr CHROMIUM	25 54.94 Mn MANGANESE	26 55.85 Fe IRON	27 58.93 Co COBALT	28 58.69 Ni NICKEL	29 63.5 Cu COPPER
5	37 85.47 Rb RUBIDIUM	38 87.62 Sr STRONTIUM	39 88.91 Y YTTRIUM	40 91.22 Zr ZIRCONIUM	41 92.91 Nb NIOBIUM	42 95.94 Mo MOLYBDENUM	43 (98) Tc TECHNETIUM	44 101.07 Ru RUTHENIUM	45 102.91 Rh RHODIUM	46 106.42 Pd PALLADIUM	47 107.8 Ag SILVER
6	55 132.91 Cs CAESIUM	56 137.33 Ba BARIUM	57 138.91 La* LANTHANUM	72 178.49 Hf HAFNIUM	73 180.95 Ta TANTALUM	74 183.85 W TUNGSTEN	75 186.21 Re RHENIUM	76 190.2 Os OSMIUM	77 192.22 Ir IRIDIUM	78 195.08 Pt PLATINUM	79 196.9 Au GOLD
7	87 (223) Fr FRANCIUM	88 (226) Ra RADIUM	89 (227) Ac** ACTINIUM	104 (257) Rf RUTHERFORDIUM	105 (260) Db DUBNIUM	106 (263) Sg SEABORGIUM	107 (262) Bh BOHRIUM	108 (265) Hs HASSIUM	109 (266) Mt MEITNERIUM	110 (271) Ds DARMSTADTIUM	111 (272 Rg ROENTGENIUM

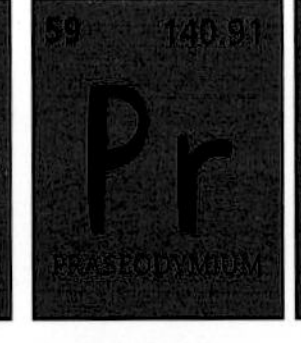

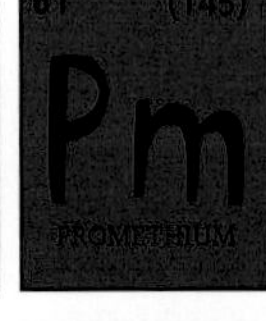

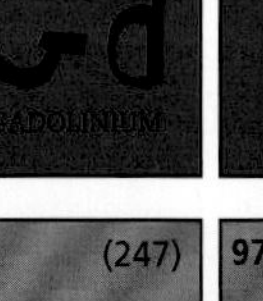

58 140.12 Ce CERIUM	59 140.91 Pr PRASEODYMIUM	60 144.24 Nd NEODYMIUM	61 (145) Pm PROMETHIUM	62 150.36 Sm SAMARIUM	63 151.96 Eu EUROPIUM	64 157.25 Gd GADOLINIUM	65 158.9 Tb TERBIUM

90 232.04 Th THORIUM	91 231.04 Pa PROTACTINIUM	92 238.03 U URANIUM	93 237.05 Np NEPTUNIUM	94 (244) Pu PLUTONIUM	95 (243) Am AMERICIUM	96 (247) Cm CURIUM	97 (247 Bk BERKELIUM

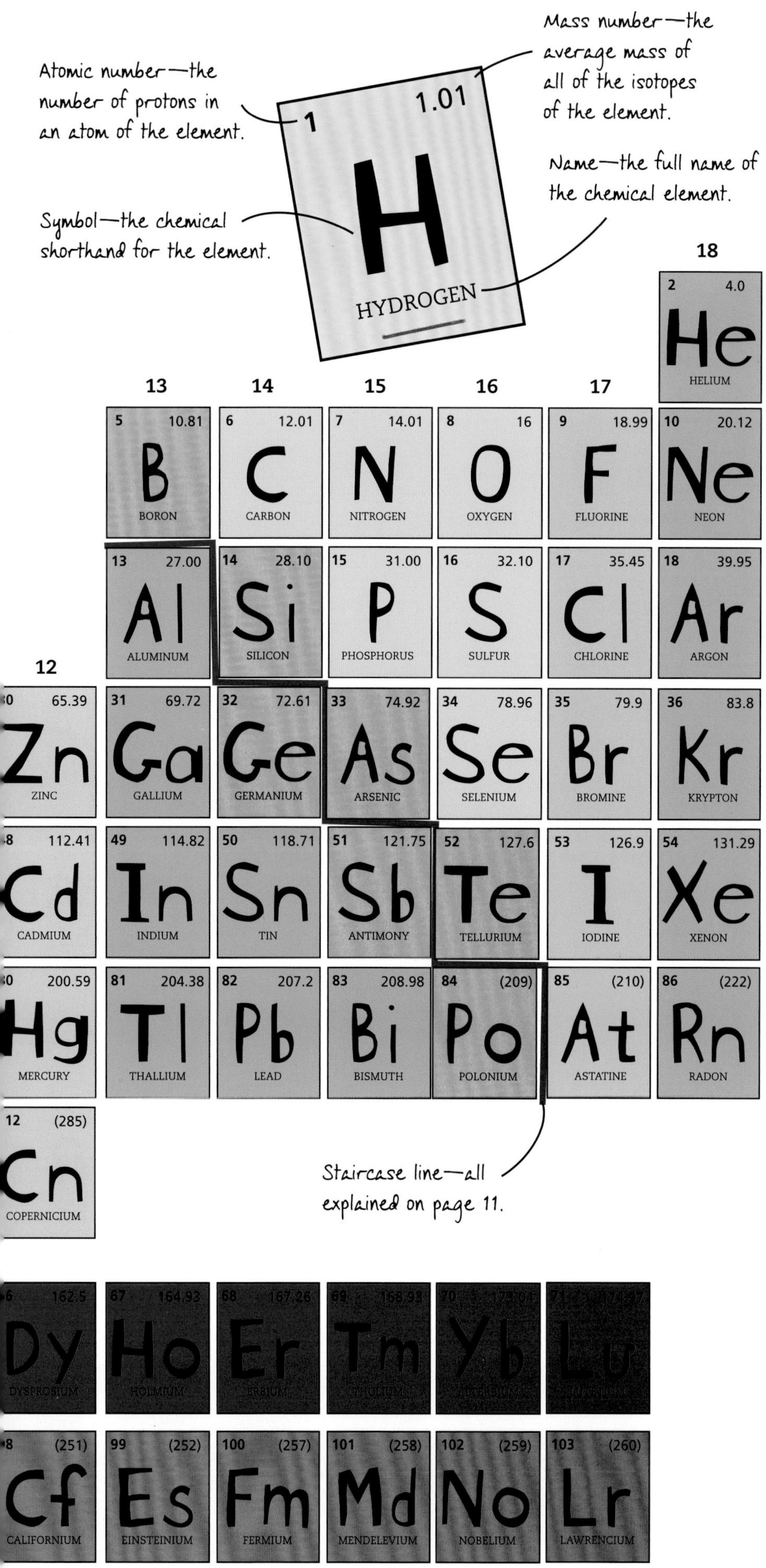

Atomic number—the number of protons in an atom of the element.

Symbol—the chemical shorthand for the element.

Mass number—the average mass of all of the isotopes of the element.

Name—the full name of the chemical element.

1	1.01
H	HYDROGEN

12	13	14	15	16	17	18
						2 4.0 He HELIUM
	5 10.81 B BORON	6 12.01 C CARBON	7 14.01 N NITROGEN	8 16 O OXYGEN	9 18.99 F FLUORINE	10 20.12 Ne NEON
	13 27.00 Al ALUMINUM	14 28.10 Si SILICON	15 31.00 P PHOSPHORUS	16 32.10 S SULFUR	17 35.45 Cl CHLORINE	18 39.95 Ar ARGON
0 65.39 Zn ZINC	31 69.72 Ga GALLIUM	32 72.61 Ge GERMANIUM	33 74.92 As ARSENIC	34 78.96 Se SELENIUM	35 79.9 Br BROMINE	36 83.8 Kr KRYPTON
8 112.41 Cd CADMIUM	49 114.82 In INDIUM	50 118.71 Sn TIN	51 121.75 Sb ANTIMONY	52 127.6 Te TELLURIUM	53 126.9 I IODINE	54 131.29 Xe XENON
0 200.59 Hg MERCURY	81 204.38 Tl THALLIUM	82 207.2 Pb LEAD	83 208.98 Bi BISMUTH	84 (209) Po POLONIUM	85 (210) At ASTATINE	86 (222) Rn RADON
12 (285) Cn COPERNICIUM						

Staircase line—all explained on page 11.

6 162.5 Dy DYSPROSIUM	67 164.93 Ho HOLMIUM	68 167.26 Er ERBIUM	69 168.93 Tm THULIUM	70 173.04 Yb YTTERBIUM	71 174.97 Lu LUTETIUM
8 (251) Cf CALIFORNIUM	99 (252) Es EINSTEINIUM	100 (257) Fm FERMIUM	101 (258) Md MENDELEVIUM	102 (259) No NOBELIUM	103 (260) Lr LAWRENCIUM

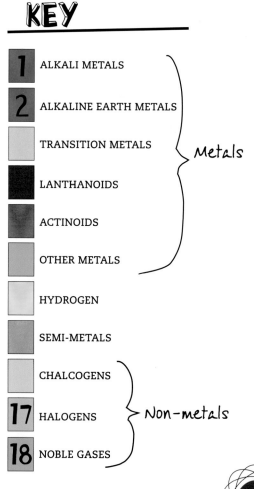

Let's form a group!

The periodic table arranges the elements into seven horizontal rows, or periods, numbered at the side, and 18 columns, or groups, numbered at the top. The chemicals in each group have the same number of electrons in their outer shell, so they tend to react in similar ways and have similar properties. Several groups have family names. The most common include:

Group 1 – The Alkali Metals
Group 2 – The Alkaline Earth Metals
Group 11 – The Coinage Metals
Group 15 – The Pnictogens
Group 16 – The Chalcogens
Group 17 – The Halogens
Group 18 – The Noble Gases

KEY

- 1 ALKALI METALS
- 2 ALKALINE EARTH METALS
- TRANSITION METALS
- LANTHANOIDS
- ACTINOIDS
- OTHER METALS

} Metals

- HYDROGEN
- SEMI-METALS
- CHALCOGENS
- 17 HALOGENS
- 18 NOBLE GASES

} Non-metals

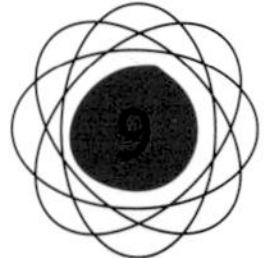

USING THE PERIODIC TABLE

The periodic table isn't just RANDOM! It's organized in a clever way that allows us to make lots of predictions about the relationships between the elements.

The periodic table gets its name from its horizontal rows, or periods. The elements in a period are not related to one another like the family members of the groups. Instead, they change gradually as you move across from left to right. One way to think of the elements in a period is like musical notes: as you pass from A to G on the scale, there is a subtle change. As you move to the next period, the pattern is repeated, like changing the pitch for another set of A–G notes at a different octave. Two whole sequences are too long to fit in the table. One of these contains elements 57–71 inclusive and are called the lanthanoids. The other contains elements 89–103, called the actinoids. Elements with atomic numbers greater than 103 are called transactinoids. The large group of metals in the middle of the periodic table are called the transition elements. They are a transition between group 2 to the left and group 13 the right.

These two sequences are usually printed below the table.

SOLID

	1	2	3	4	5	6	7	8	9	10	11	12	13	14	15	16	17	18
1	H																	He
2	Li	Be											B	C	N	O	F	Ne
3	Na	Mg											Al	Si	P	S	Cl	Ar
4	K	Ca	Sc	Ti	V	Cr	Mn	Fe	Co	Ni	Cu	Zn	Ga	Ge	As	Se	Br	Kr
5	Rb	Sr	Y	Zr	Nb	Mo	Tc	Ru	Rh	Pd	Ag	Cd	In	Sn	Sb	Te	I	Xe
6	Cs	Ba	La*	Hf	Ta	W	Re	Os	Ir	Pt	Au	Hg	Tl	Pb	Bi	Po	At	Rn
7	Fr	Ra	Ac**	Rf	Db	Sg	Bh	Hs	Mt	Ds	Rg	Cn						

Ce	Pr	Nd	Pm	Sm	Eu	Gd	Tb	Dy	Ho	Er	Tm	Yb	Lu
Th	Pa	U	Np	Pu	Am	Cm	Bk	Cf	Es	Fm	Md	No	Lr

LIQUID

Metals, non-metals, and metalloids

Another way to classify the elements, apart from by group and period, is to sort them into metals and non-metals.

Most of the elements on the periodic table are metals:
Metals can be recognized as having lustre (they are shiny), as being good conductors of heat and electricity, and as being malleable (they can be shaped) and ductile (they can be drawn out into thin wires). Metals are usually solids at room temperature but, as you probably know already, mercury is a liquid metal.
Non-metals are poor conductors of heat and electricity and can be liquids and gases as well as solids at room temperature. They are not usually shiny and are not malleable or ductile.
Metalloids (or semi-metals) are elements that can act like a cross between metals and non-metals.

The metals and non-metals are separated by the "staircase line" on the periodic table that starts beneath boron (B) and winds its way down between polonium (Po) and astatine (At): the metals are to the left of the staircase, and the non-metals are to the right. Many of the elements touching the line are considered metalloids.

Elements exist in three states: solid, liquid, and gas. Most of the elements on the periodic table are solids at room temperature. In fact, only two are liquids (bromine and mercury), and a handful are gases, like oxygen, hydrogen, nitrogen, fluorine, chlorine, and the noble gases.

Substances change state according to temperature and pressure, by melting, evaporating, condensing, or freezing.

BRAIN BOX

WHO'S THE DADDY?

Dmitri Mendeleev (1834–1907)

When it comes to organizing the elements, the daddy of them all is the Russian chemist Dmitri Mendeleev. Generally accepted as the "father" of the modern periodic table, Mendeleev was a genius at successfully bringing together earlier attempts to arrange the elements. Not only did he arrange them—he even left gaps where as-yet undiscovered elements would eventually fit. In 1869 he presented his ideas to the Russian Chemical Society, and the periodic table was born. And today the gaps have been filled, just as Mendeleev predicted!

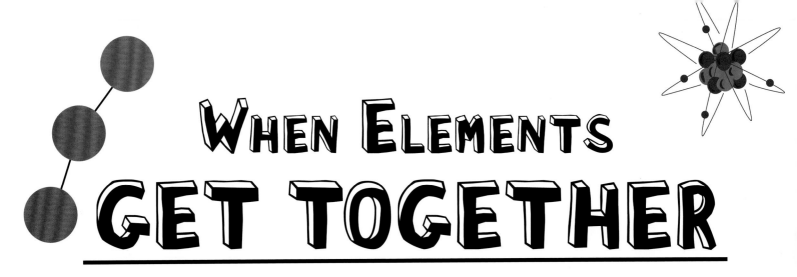

WHEN ELEMENTS GET TOGETHER

All of the things you'll read about in this book are made up of the elements on the periodic table, but they can come together in many different ways.

Atoms, molecules, and compounds

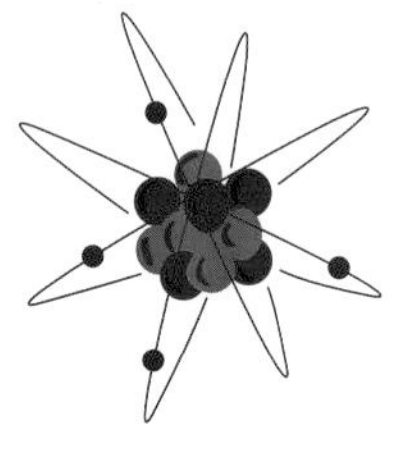

Sometimes the atoms of an element go around on their own—they are loners. One example is mercury (Hg), which was used in old thermometers. Sometimes atoms form small groups called molecules. Many common gases go around in pairs, like O_2, N_2, and H_2, while other elements form larger groups where molecules have more than two atoms, like P_4 and S_8 for phosphorus and sulfur. In molecules, atoms are bonded together by sharing electrons; this type of bonding is called covalent.

Elements form compounds more often than they exist on their own.

Usually, elements combine to make compounds. In a compound, elements bond together in fixed amounts. For example, water is a compound: it always has two hydrogen atoms connected to an oxygen atom (H_2O). In a molecule of water, the atoms are bonded by sharing electrons, so it is a covalent compound.

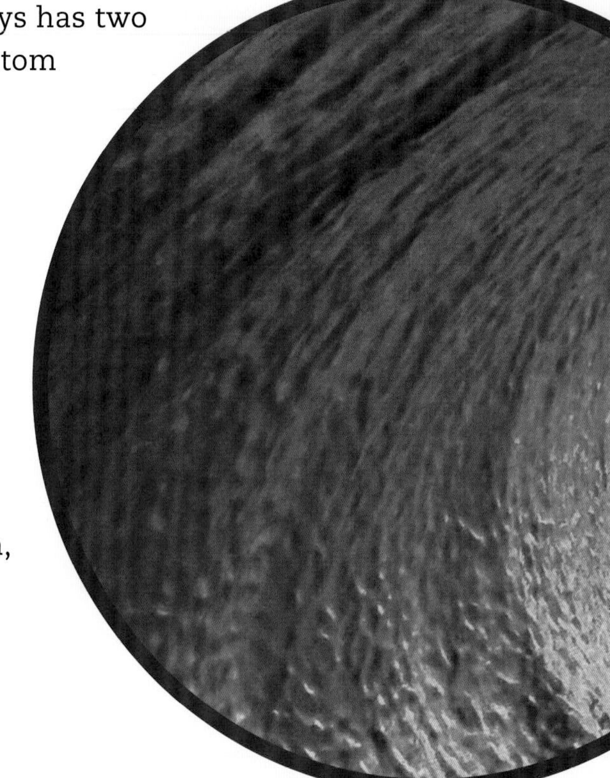

Ions

In another form of bonding, elements do not share electrons. Instead, electrons are transferred from one atom to another. All atoms are neutral: they have as many positive protons as negative electrons. If an atom loses an electron to another atom, then the atoms are no longer neutral.

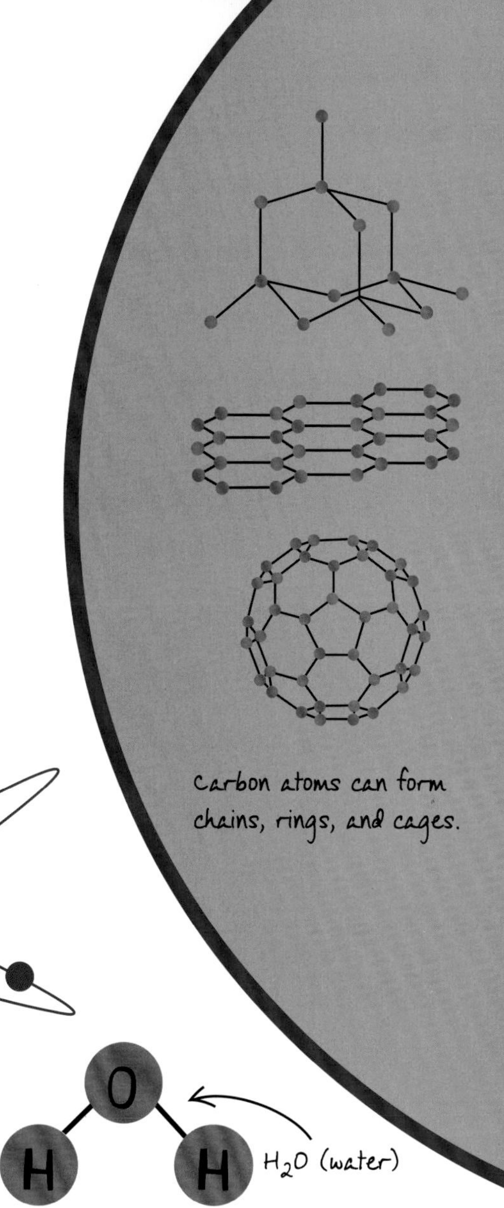

Carbon atoms can form chains, rings, and cages.

Carbon loves ITSELF!

Look at me, look at me! Boy oh boy, that carbon is one self-absorbed element. Unlike many other elements, carbon atoms can form lots of covalent chemical bonds with themselves. That means that carbon can form chains, rings, and cages made up of carbon atoms. These molecular compounds of carbon can be anything from just a few atoms long all the way up to absolutely HUGE numbers, with thousands and thousands of atoms present. EXTREMELY long chains are called polymers (no, nothing to do with Polly the parrot, but "poly" meaning "many"). Hanging off these chains and rings are many other atoms that come along for the ride. These joyriders are mainly hydrogen, oxygen, and nitrogen, but also include atoms like sulfur, phosphorus, and the halogens.

The chemistry of carbon compounds is called ORGANIC chemistry. Most organic chemistry is tied up in the biology of living things, or things that are now dead but were once alive. It is such an important branch of chemistry that there is a whole sub-science devoted to it. You already know lots of organic compounds, even if you don't recognize all of the names. Sugars (carbohydrates or "carbs"), proteins, and fats are all organic molecules, as are most plastics (they contain organic polymers). MEGA-important biological molecules are all organic, too, like DNA (Deoxyribonucleic acid), which provides the blueprint for all LIFE.

CO_2 (carbon dioxide)

In ionic bonds, opposite charges attract.

The atom that loses an electron will have a positive charge, and the other will have a negative charge. Charged particles are called IONS, and the attraction between the opposite charges is called an IONIC bond. An example of an ionic compound is table salt or sodium chloride, NaCl. In NaCl, one sodium positive ion is combined with one chloride negative ion. Compounds made between metals and non-metals often have ionic bonds.

The type of bonding and the way that the atoms in an element, molecule, or compound are arranged greatly influences the properties of a chemical substance and therefore its uses. For example, ionic bonds are very strong, so ionic compounds tend to have high melting and boiling points and may be used where heat resistance is important, for instance in lining furnaces.

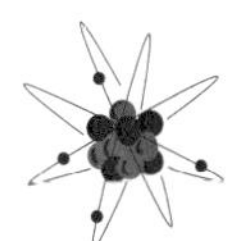

Pm
Cl
Si
Anyone seen any cavemen?
F
Al
U
Kr
I'm LOST!
Be

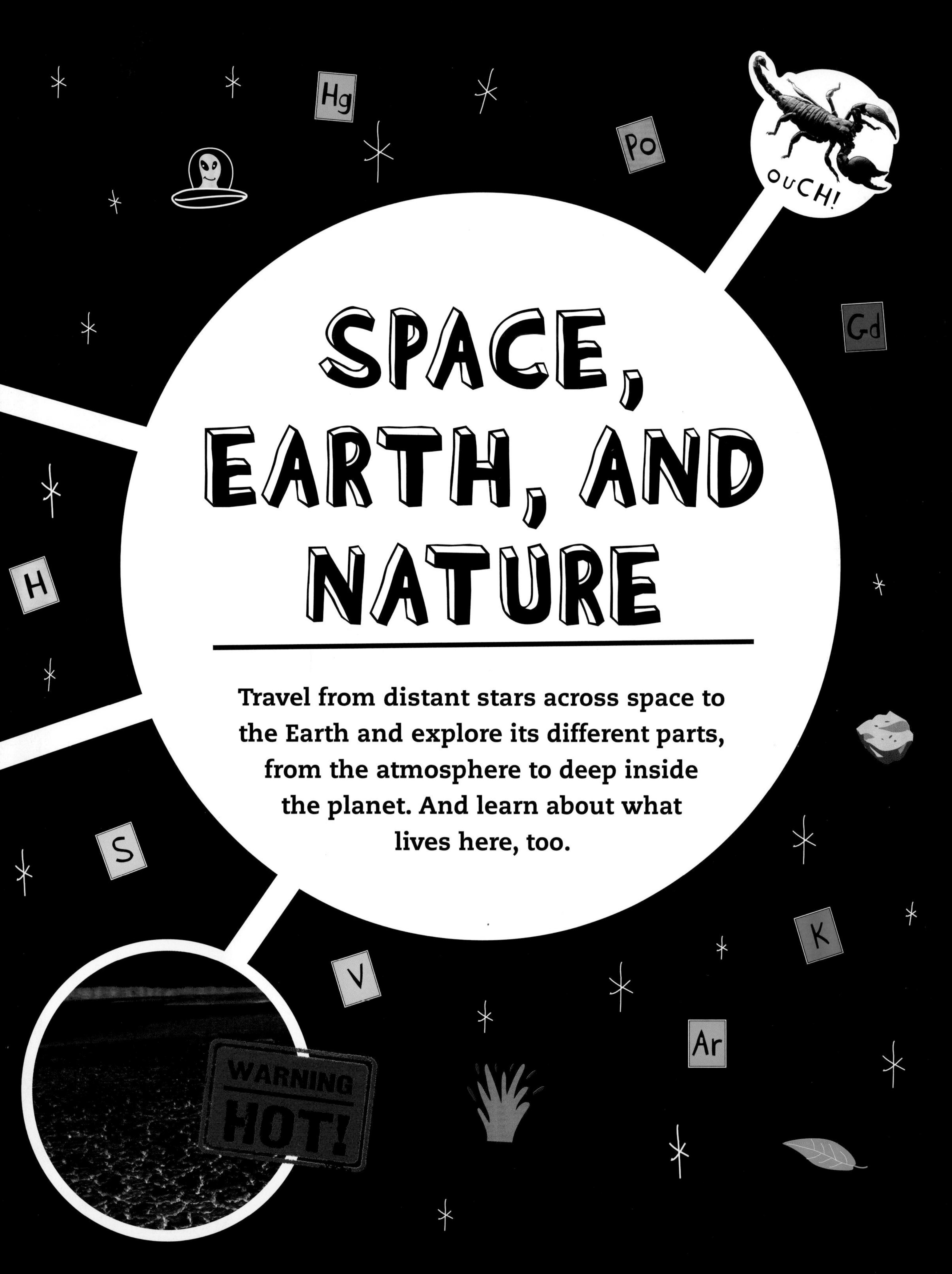

SPACE, EARTH, AND NATURE

Travel from distant stars across space to the Earth and explore its different parts, from the atmosphere to deep inside the planet. And learn about what lives here, too.

I'M GONNA MAKE YOU A STAR

Stars are cool. Of course, they're also VERY hot. Without our nearest star, the Sun, there would be no life on Earth (and you wouldn't be reading this).

Stars are massive collections of hot plasma. They form in space when hydrogen and helium nuclei (and a few heavier elements like oxygen and carbon) collapse in on themselves to create a huge ball of really hot gas. Inside the star, nuclear reactions take place where new elements are formed. In the process, HUGE amounts of energy are released. In time the pressure and temperatures at the star's center grow, and lots of other nuclear reactions can take place, forming many other elements such as silicon, magnesium, sulfur, and even iron.

Plasma is the term used in physics and chemistry for a gas that contains lots of charged particles or ions.

WHAT'S IT MADE OF?

hydrogen, helium, oxygen, carbon, silicon, magnesium, sulfur, iron

Elementary stuff

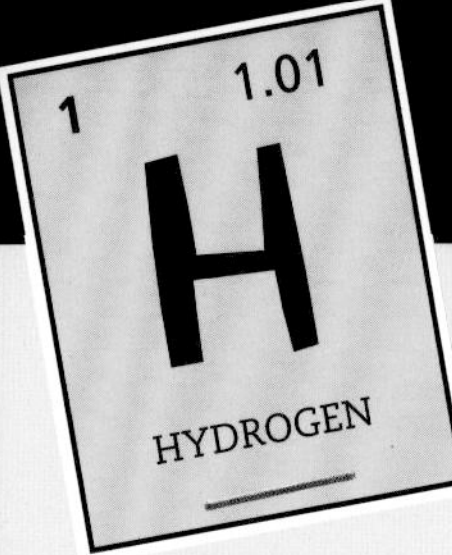

- **Atomic Number: 1**
- Atomic Mass: 1.01
- **Isotopes: 3 naturally occurring isotopes**
- Boiling Point: –423˚F (–253˚C)
- **Melting Point: –434˚F (–259˚C)**

Hydrogen

Around 90 percent of all atoms in the universe are hydrogen atoms. It is the fuel that makes stars glow. It is the lightest of all gases, and one of the most reactive. It usually occurs on Earth in combination with other elements, especially with oxygen—as water. It is also a basic element of life, with carbon and oxygen.

Learning about stars

No one has ever been to a star, of course. We know about them from the light they give off. The light reveals which elements are inside, the star's temperature, and even its age.

Cork ROCKET

You could fly among the stars with a rocket...but don't get TOO close! SAFETY TIP: Flying corks can be dangerous, so wear some eye protection!

WHAT YOU'LL NEED

- baking soda
- 4 fl. oz. (120 mL) lemon juice
- a small plastic bottle
- a cork
- water
- toilet paper
- thread

1. Take a large piece of toilet paper and put a tablespoon (15 g) of baking soda in the middle. Wrap the toilet paper around the baking soda and tie it up with a piece of thread to make a small packet.
2. Put the lemon juice into the bottom of the bottle.
3. Add water carefully to the bottle by pouring it gently down the inside walls until the bottle is about half full.
4. Drop in the baking soda packet and quickly pop in the cork.
5. Shake the bottle, place it on the ground, and stand back!
6. Repeat using 4 fl. oz. (120 mL) vinegar or cola in place of the lemon juice.

How does that work?: Baking soda is a chemical called sodium hydrogen carbonate. Lemon juice, vinegar, and cola all contain acids. When carbonates react with acids they produce carbon dioxide gas. The gas increases the pressure inside the bottle until it eventually blows out the cork!

WARNING
VERY HOT!!

When a star's nuclei fuse, some of their mass is converted to energy as heat! LOTS and LOTS of heat!

De-confusing fusion

About 98–99 percent of the sun is made up of only two elements, hydrogen and helium. Hydrogen nuclei crash into one another and "fuse" or join together. In the process they create helium and release a massive amount of energy. Also present in stars are oxygen, carbon, nitrogen, silicon, magnesium, neon, iron, and sulfur.

HOME, SWEET HOME

Take off from the Sun and head for the third big rock you see. One of the eight planets in our solar system, Earth is easy to spot: it's the only one with life...so far!

What on EARTH?

It's quite hard to miss the Earth. It is one big, big, BIG rock—ginormous. The planet weighs approximately 13 x 10^{24} lb. (6 x 10^{24} kg). That's a scientific way of saying 13 with 24 zeros, or 13,000,000,000,000,000,000,000,000 lb.!! Try finding a set of scales to weigh THAT!

In the air: The air we breathe contains lots of gases, like nitrogen (78 percent of regular air) and oxygen (21 percent). In other layers of the atmosphere, we find other gases like carbon dioxide (CO_2), methane (CH_4), and ozone (a wacky form of triplet oxygen atoms, O_3). See "The Atmosphere" on page 20 for more information.

All at sea

Around 71 percent of Earth is covered with water. Water means plenty of hydrogen and oxygen in the form of H_2O, but the oceans contain a huge number of other elements, too. These elements are found in the oceans dissolved as salts, so don't go looking for a big lump of metal floating around in the sea!

TOP 10 sea ELEMENTS

Na

The TOP 10 elements found underwater are: chlorine, sodium, magnesium, sulfur, calcium, potassium, bromine, carbon, strontium, and boron.

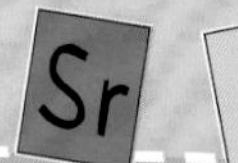

S

Earth's top 10

Depending on how you count them and who you ask, there are around 92 naturally occuring elements on Earth. The rocks that make up the crust of the Earth are almost all oxides of these elements, rather than pure elements, since oxygen gas tends to react with the abundant elements to form compounds.

Oxides are compounds formed when elements combine with oxygen.

Abundance is the measure of how much stuff there is.

Top 10 Earth ELEMENTS

The Top 10 elements in terms of their abundance are: oxygen, silicon, aluminium, iron, calcium, sodium, potassium, magnesium, titanium, and hydrogen.

TOP 10 Air ELEMENTS

The TOP 10 elements in the atmosphere are: nitrogen, oxygen, argon, neon, helium, krypton, hydrogen, xenon, radon, and chlorine.

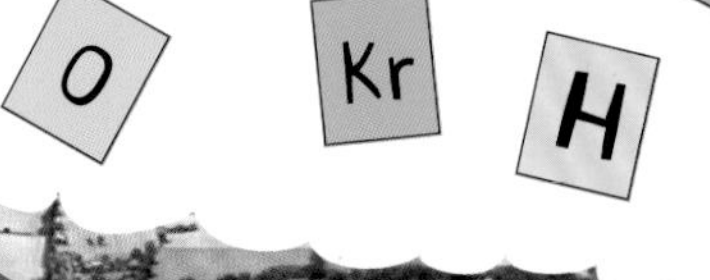

WHAT'S IT MADE OF?

All the elements! (at least all 92 naturally occuring ones!)

Really COOL Science Bit

Lay(er) it on me!

Like the atmosphere, the Earth itself is made up of a series of layers that, when named from the center outward, are called the inner core, the outer core, the mantle, the upper mantle, and the crust. The main body of the Earth is made of rock (see "Let's Rock," page 22). The final outer layer is called the pedosphere. We usually just call the pedosphere "soil" (well, it's easier to say!).

The Atmosphere

An atmosphere is a ball of gases that surrounds a planet. It's held in place by gravity. Without Earth's atmosphere, we wouldn't only die from a lack of air—we would all be TOAST!

If Earth's atmosphere ever vanished it might be possible to make a new one, but only with lots of supplies and a VERY large space. The job would need a kitchen or workshop with a ceiling at least 62 mi. (100 km) high! Air is made up of a few elements and also some compounds. So 99 percent of the room is going to be filled with the elements nitrogen (78 percent) and oxygen (21 percent). The other 1 percent will be a mixture of elements like krypton, helium, and neon, and some compounds like carbon dioxide and water vapor. Until the mixture was ready, everyone would need to wear SCUBA gear because without air you cannot breathe.

Helium is lighter than most gases, so it's great for filling balloons.

WHAT'S IT MADE OF?

Lots of oxygen, nitrogen, argon, carbon; plus smaller amounts of neon, helium, hydrogen, krypton

Really COOL Science Bit

A far, far NOBLER thing...

The noble gases is the collective name for the elements in group 18 of the periodic table: helium, neon, argon, krypton, xenon, and radon. They hang out on their own in an exclusive area on the right-hand side of the table. These elements were originally thought to be inert (unreactive) and aloof—like noble aristocrats who would not mix with common folk (like the other elements). It has since been found that some of these elements DO actually mix with the riffraff of the periodic table to form some compounds.

BRAIN BOX

REVELATION...AND REVOLUTION!

Antoine–Laurent Lavoisier (1743–1794)

Born into the French aristocracy, Lavoisier achieved a lot in a short time. In 1789 he wrote *Elementary Treatise of Chemistry,* which is often seen as the first modern chemistry textbook. It included a list of the elements known at the time, including hydrogen and oxygen. Lavoisier was most famous for his law of conservation of mass. It overturned an old theory that all flammable material contained an element called phlogiston, which was released by burning. Lavoisier was pretty smart, but he could not save himself. He was beheaded as a traitor in the French Revolution.

WHOOSH!

KARMAN LINE: Theodore von Karman, a Hungarian-born physicist, calculated that normal aircraft could not function above this height, and that this was the end of the atmosphere and the beginning of outer space.
EXOSPHERE
THERMOSPHERE
MESOSPHERE
STRATOSPHERE
TROPOSPHERE
OUCH!
62 mi. (100 km)
50 mi. (80 km)
31 mi. (50 km)
6 mi. (10 km)

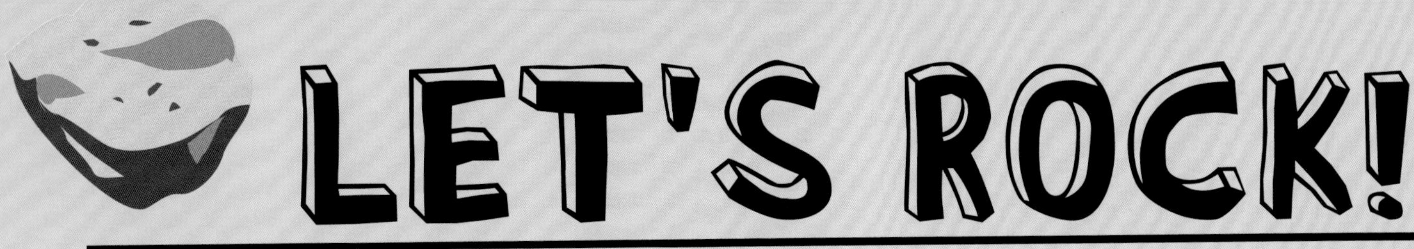

LET'S ROCK!

Rocks played a huge part in our past. When our ancestors didn't have anything else to use, rocks provided them with tools and weapons.

What are rocks?

If you look in a dictionary, the definition will describe a rock as something like "an aggregate of minerals." This just means that it's a bunch of chemicals tightly packed together to give a solid (usually hard) material. The science of studying rocks is called petrology, but when we are talking about the rocks and other materials, like liquids, that make up Earth, we call it geology.

An aggregate is a load of particles squeezed together.

Not the same as rock candy—that's all sugar!

WHAT'S IT MADE OF?

All 92 naturally occurring elements!

Stone cold facts

The Earth has a hard outer layer called the lithosphere; *lithos* is a Greek word meaning "stone" or "rock." Because rocks are made up of literally thousands of different minerals and chemical compounds, it is difficult to shorten the list of naturally occurring elements that make up rocks. It's possible to argue that all 92 naturally occurring elements are present. The top 10 in order of decreasing abundance in Earth's crust are: oxygen, silicon, aluminium, iron, calcium, sodium, potassium, magnesium, titanium, and hydrogen.

basalt

sandstone

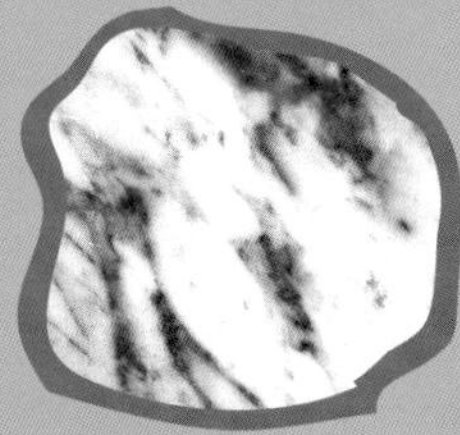

marble

Three types

Any geologist or petrologist worth his or her salt (get it?!) knows that there are three different types of rock. **Igneous** rocks are those that are formed as a result of some volcanic magma or lava cooling down. Examples include granite and basalt. **Sedimentary** rocks are those formed when tiny particles (or sediments) settle in one place and are then packed together to form layers of material that become rocks. An example is sandstone. **Metamorphic** rocks are those that are formed through extreme changes in temperature and pressure inside the Earth. Slate and marble are examples of such rocks.

Rock of Ages

Rocks are pretty tough—some of the oldest rocks on Earth are estimated to be about 4 BILLION years old. That's OLD! Before humans worked out how to extract metals from the ground, they used rocks for all sorts of purposes. That period of history is usually called the "Stone Age." See if you can guess why.

DON'T BLOW YOUR TOP!

The word "volcano" comes from the name of the Roman god Vulcan, who used volcanoes as furnaces for his iron work. The Romans were right about one thing: volcanoes are very, very hot.

RUMBLE!

Magma and lava

The molten rock that volcanoes spew out is called lava. When it is still deep beneath the ground, lava is known as magma. The magma is INCREDIBLY hot—hot enough to melt metal! The chemical compositions of magma and lava are complicated, but both have silicon dioxide (SiO_2) as their main ingredient. The other major components include magnesium and iron oxides. Since the two most abundant elements in Earth's crust are oxygen and silicon, it's no surprise that when a volcano blasts parts of the crust into the atmosphere a large part of what is thrown up takes the form of silicon dioxide!

Magma reaches between 1,300 and 2,400°F (700 to 1,300°C).

Gas explosion

As well as molten lava, volcanoes blast out loads of gases. The clouds rise miles into the atmosphere. Typical volcanoes produce large amounts of H_2O (water vapor), CO_2 (carbon dioxide), and SO_2 (sulfur dioxide) as well as smaller amounts of gases such as H_2S (hydrogen sulfide), H_2 (hydrogen), CO (carbon monoxide), HCl (hydrogen chloride), and HF (hydrogen fluoride).

SpLat!

TRY THIS

Table-top VOLCANO

A little less dangerous than the real thing…but pretty spectacular!

WHAT YOU'LL NEED

plastic water bottle
3 1/3 cups (825 g) flour
2 cups (500 mL) water
vegetable oil
2 1/2 cups (625 g) salt
disposable foil tray
liquid dish detergent
baking soda
white vinegar

1. Take the water and add the flour and salt and some vegetable oil. Knead the ingredients together to make a dough.
2. Stand the bottle in the foil baking tray.
3. Using the bottle as a mold, use the dough to form your volcano shape around it. Don't cover the top of the bottle. Score some lines into the dough to make "lava tracks."
4. Add warm water to almost fill the bottle and then add a generous squirt of dish detergent.
5. Add 2 tbsp. (30 g) of baking soda to the bottle.
6. Slowly pour the vinegar into the bottle.

What makes it work? **Baking soda is a chemical called sodium hydrogen carbonate. Vinegar contains ethanoic acid. When carbonates react with acids they produce carbon-dioxide gas. As the gas is produced it escapes from the inside of the "volcano" and brings the soapy bubbles out with it.**

HISS!

Many other complex mixtures of gases are possible, too. Because magma is viscous, gases can suddenly explode through it. That causes a huge shower of boiling hot rocks! Many volcanic gases dissolve in the water present in clouds to produce acids; so any rain that falls close to a volcanic eruption falls as acid rain, which can be extremely corrosive.

WHAT'S IT MADE OF? silicon, oxygen, magnesium, carbon, hydrogen, sulfur, chlorine, nitrogen, fluorine, iron

What makes the ground move?

Ancient Hawaiians believed that the goddess Pele made volcanoes erupt when she was angry and caused earthquakes by stomping her feet! Even today science doesn't have all of the answers about these phenomena. So you never know…other forces may still be at work beneath the ground!

WARNING HOT!

Lost in the DESERT

A desert isn't defined by what it's made of, but by what's missing! What makes a desert a desert isn't sand or sunshine (or even camels), but the lack of one chemical substance: H_2O.

Say NO to H_2O

A desert receives less than 10 in. (250 mm) of rain per year. Another way to define a desert is a place where more water is lost by evaporation than is gained by precipitation.

Evaporation occurs when liquid particles turn into gas; the opposite process (gas turning into liquid) is called condensation.

Precipitation is the natural condensation of the Earth's water vapor—that usually means rain, hail, or snow.

Life's a beach

There may not be much H_2O in deserts, but there is still plenty of oxygen that comes from a different compound. Sand is a bunch of rock and mineral particles mainly made up of silica or silicon dioxide (SiO_2). Oxygen and silicon are the number 1 and number 2 elements found in the Earth's crust, partly because of all the silicon dioxide in desert sand.

I'm thirsty!

Careful!—Safety Tip

Don't bother taking a bucket and spade. Desert sand is too dry to build sandcastles. And never, ever BURY your dad in a sand dune while he's asleep. You might NEVER find him again!

WHAT'S IT MADE OF?

silicon, oxygen, sodium, calcium, sulfur, nitrogen, chlorine, boron

Really COOL Science Bit

Hot or cold?

Deserts cover about one-third of the whole surface of the Earth, but they're not always HOT. A desert can be hot or cold, and sometimes it's BOTH! Even hot deserts like the Sahara get really cold at night. The temperatures can be over 110°F (43°C) during the day but fall to less than freezing (32°F / 0°C) at night. The two largest deserts on Earth are the frozen deserts at the Poles, where there is very little precipitation. The South Pole is at the center of the Antarctic region, and the North Pole is at the heart of the frozen Arctic ocean. The largest hot desert in the world is the Sahara, which stretches across a huge area of North Africa and is part of several different countries.

DANGER
A BAD PLACE TO TAKE A WALK!

Hold the water!

Many minerals are found in the deposits left by the evaporation of water in deserts. The most common are calcium sulfate (often called gypsum) and others including sodium nitrate, sodium chloride, and lots of borates (compounds that include boron and oxygen). Some of these minerals are pretty useful. Gypsum is used to make plaster for building. Sodium nitrate is used to make fertilizers and solid fuel for rockets.

I think I can see an ice-cream truck!

HOME DECORATION FOR CAVEMEN

The ground feels solid, right? Wrong! Under your feet, Earth changes all the time. It's difficult to see this underground chemistry in action, but caves can give us a glimpse of it.

Up or down?

Stalagmites form on the floors of caves. They "grow" upward when water drips from the roof of the cave and deposits minerals on top of them. Stalactites hang from the ceilings of caves and are made in the same way. How can you remember which is which? Easy: a stalactite clings TIGHT to the ceiling, while a stalagmite MIGHT grow as tall as a person. When a stalagmite and stalactite meet, they form what's known as a column.

Underground water carries minerals dissolved as salts, like sea water. See page 32.

Water underground contains many hundreds of different, dissolved elements and their compounds. The simplest way to think of the process is in a number of steps.

State symbols

The equations on the opposite page use some lowercase letters in parentheses. Don't worry—they're not as scary as they look! The letters just tell us which state of matter a chemical is in. The (s) stands for solid, (l) means liquid, (g) shows a gas is present, and (aq) means something is dissolved in water—it stands for "aqueous" from the Latin *aqua* meaning "water." So the equations show us that stalagmites and stalactites are SOLID calcium carbonate.

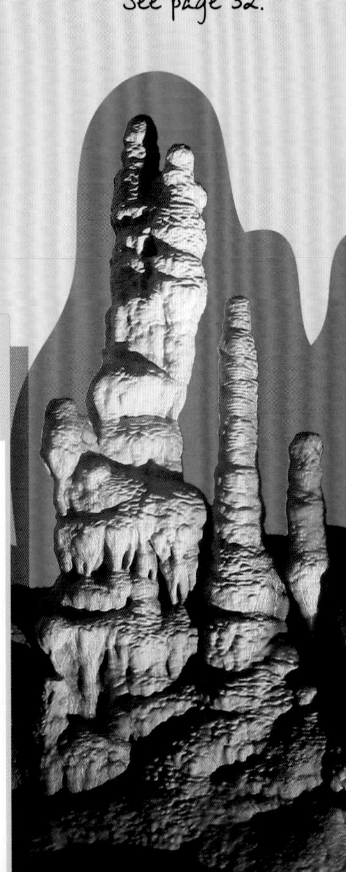

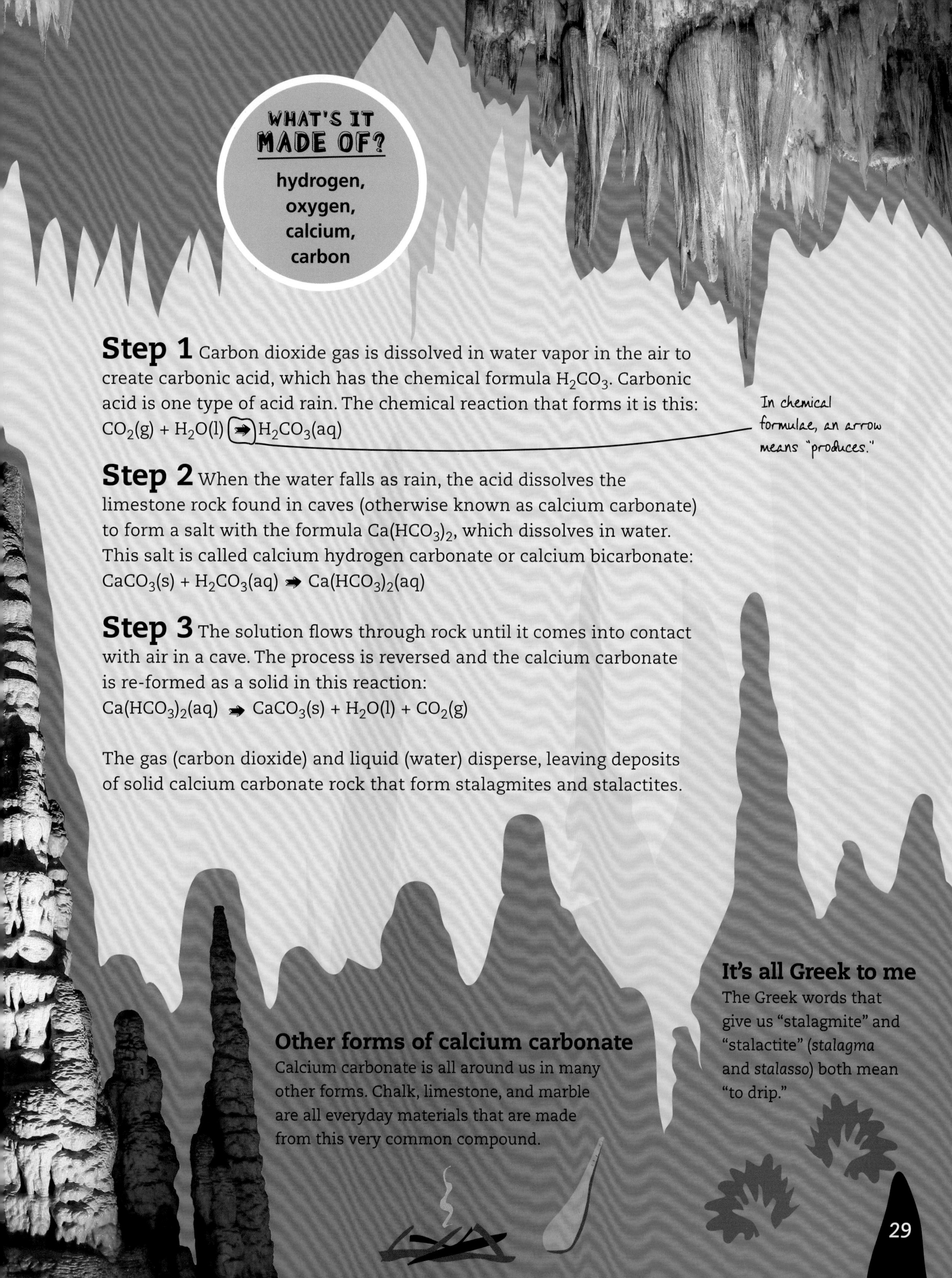

WHAT'S IT MADE OF?

hydrogen, oxygen, calcium, carbon

Step 1 Carbon dioxide gas is dissolved in water vapor in the air to create carbonic acid, which has the chemical formula H_2CO_3. Carbonic acid is one type of acid rain. The chemical reaction that forms it is this:
$CO_2(g) + H_2O(l) \rightarrow H_2CO_3(aq)$

In chemical formulae, an arrow means "produces."

Step 2 When the water falls as rain, the acid dissolves the limestone rock found in caves (otherwise known as calcium carbonate) to form a salt with the formula $Ca(HCO_3)_2$, which dissolves in water. This salt is called calcium hydrogen carbonate or calcium bicarbonate:
$CaCO_3(s) + H_2CO_3(aq) \rightarrow Ca(HCO_3)_2(aq)$

Step 3 The solution flows through rock until it comes into contact with air in a cave. The process is reversed and the calcium carbonate is re-formed as a solid in this reaction:
$Ca(HCO_3)_2(aq) \rightarrow CaCO_3(s) + H_2O(l) + CO_2(g)$

The gas (carbon dioxide) and liquid (water) disperse, leaving deposits of solid calcium carbonate rock that form stalagmites and stalactites.

Other forms of calcium carbonate

Calcium carbonate is all around us in many other forms. Chalk, limestone, and marble are all everyday materials that are made from this very common compound.

It's all Greek to me

The Greek words that give us "stalagmite" and "stalactite" (*stalagma* and *stalasso*) both mean "to drip."

Catch Your COMET!

It's not much fun being a comet. Your lonely orbits of the Sun take you into freezing space beyond the solar system. And when you pass close to Earth, everyone wants to stare at you.

WARNING VERY COLD!!

HUGE, dirty snowballs!

Astronomers love comets. They hope that they will provide clues about the chemistry of the solar system and how it formed.

A comet contains rock, dust, ice, hydrogen gas, and many other frozen gases, such as carbon dioxide, carbon monoxide, methane, and ammonia. They also contain many organic compounds (compounds of carbon) like methanol, ethanol, aldehydes, and amino acids, plus all kinds of other hydrocarbon compounds.

The ice part of comets means that astronomers sometimes call them "dirty snowballs"!

WHAT'S IT MADE OF?

carbon, hydrogen, oxygen, nitrogen

WHIZZ!

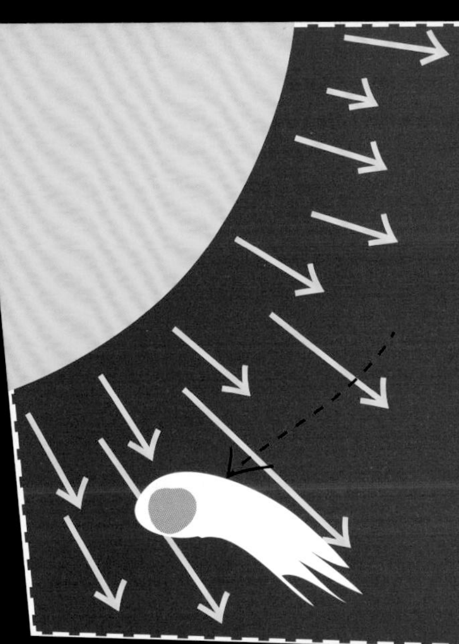

SOLAR Wind

The word "comet" comes from a Greek word meaning "head of hair." Er... what does THAT mean? Well, when a comet is visible from Earth it often produces a "tail" of debris that sometimes looks like long hair flowing in the wind! The tail is formed when the comet gets close enough to the Sun for some of its material to melt and turn into dust and gas. The Sun produces solar wind, which is a stream of energy that blows the tiny dust and gas particles into the shape of a tail. Solar wind always blows away from the Sun, so if the comet is moving away from the Sun as well, its "tail" actually blows along in front of it! Weird! Eventually a comet will melt completely and disappear.

Celebrity comets

You may have heard of Halley's comet, which has become the best known of this type of celestial body. It was named after English astronomer Edmund Halley and it can be seen from Earth every 75 years or so. It is next scheduled to appear in 2061, so you have some time to wait if you want to see it! Another famous comet was discovered in the late part of the 20th century. The Hale–Bopp comet was discovered in 1995 and was at its brightest in 1997. It won't be back for at least another 2,000 years—so there's not much point hanging around to see that one!

Halley predicted in 1705 that his comet would return in 1758. It did, but he wasn't around to see it—he would have had to live to 102!

Comet OR meteor?

Comets and meteors are both small solar system bodies (SSSB), but comets are much bigger. They also have tails. Comets orbit the Sun, while meteors just drift in space. A meteor is called a meteorite if it falls to Earth. Lots of meteors together sometimes form a great spectacle called a meteor shower!

OCEANS & SEAS

You might have heard Earth called the "Blue Planet." Over two-thirds of it is covered in water. This isn't pure H_2O, though. Seawater is full of other elements and compounds.

Oceans (huge bodies of water) and seas (smaller bodies of water) cover about 70 percent of Earth's surface. They contain water that is described as saline. This means that the water has salts dissolved in it. Most people usually think of the word "salt" as meaning just regular old table salt or sodium chloride. In fact, "salt" has a far wider meaning in chemistry. Sodium chloride is just one example of a much larger group of compounds that chemists call "salts" (see box below).

Ahoy!

Don't drink the water!

The salts in seawater, especially the sodium chloride, make it unsuitable for drinking. The sodium ions can build up in the body to toxic levels. They also cause the body to excrete more and more of the sodium via urinating. This kind of defeats the object of drinking the water because it means that the more seawater you drink, the thirstier you are likely to get.

On average, every quart (liter) of seawater contains about 1.2 oz. (35 g) of various salts.

It's NOT just sodium chloride!

Salts are compounds formed when the hydrogen ions in an acid are replaced by another positive ion (usually a metal ion). For example, hydrochloric acid has the formula HCl, so when the hydrogen ion is replaced by a sodium ion, we get a compound with the formula NaCl or sodium chloride. If the acid were nitric acid (HNO_3), and we replaced the hydrogen ion with a potassium ion, we would get KNO_3, which is the salt potassium nitrate. Many thousands of other combinations of positive ions replacing hydrogen ions are possible, so there are many thousands of "salts"—and most of them occur in seawater!

Eventually your kidneys will fail and death can follow! This problem is what inspired the poet Samuel Taylor Coleridge's line in his famous poem "The Rime of the Ancient Mariner," about sailors adrift at sea: "Water, water, everywhere, Nor any drop to drink."

Charging around

Ions are the particles that make up any salt, and they carry either a positive or negative charge. The ions come together to make the salts electrically neutral, meaning that they have no overall charge. The positives cancel out the oppositely charged negatives and vice-versa. In sodium chloride the positive ion is sodium, Na^+, and the negative ion is chloride, Cl^-. Since there are so many different salts, there are also lots of different types of ions in the oceans. Typically you can find all of these ions in seawater: Cl^-, Na^+, Mg^{2+}, SO_4^{2-}, Ca^{2+}, K^+, Br^-, Sr^{2+}, and F^-. You'll also find many other elements, such as carbon and boron in the form of carbonate salts (CO_3^{2-}) and borates like BO_3^{3-}.

The WORLD OCEAN and the HYDROSPHERE

Although we tend to think of the Pacific, Indian, Arctic, Southern, and Atlantic Oceans as separate bodies of water, in reality they are all connected together in one continuous body. This idea is sometimes called the World Ocean. Together the oceans form the largest part of the Earth's hydrosphere. The hydrosphere is the system that includes all the water that exists under, on, and above the surface of the planet and controls the weather and the water cycle that sustains life on Earth.

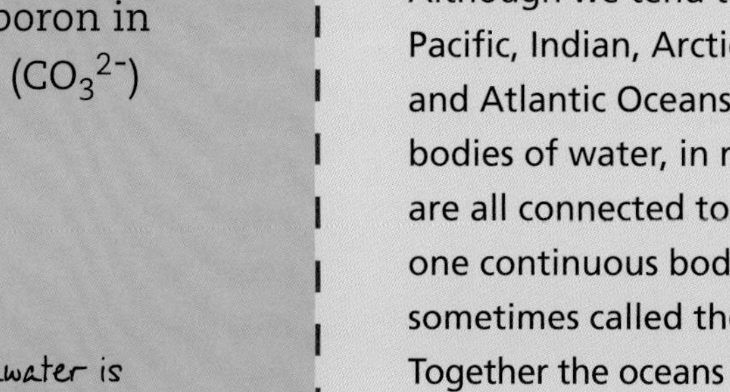

Seawater is also full of living things—mostly in the form of billions of invisible viruses. Yuck!

Seeing Blue? The oceans are generally thought of as being "blue." In fact, they only appear blue because the water absorbs red light and reflects blue.

WHAT'S IT MADE OF?

sodium, chlorine, magnesium, strontium, fluorine, bromine, calcium, sulfur, hydrogen, carbon, boron

Make Your Own Human Being

If your parents are being too strict or they won't drive you where you need to go, here's a perfect answer: make your own grown-up!

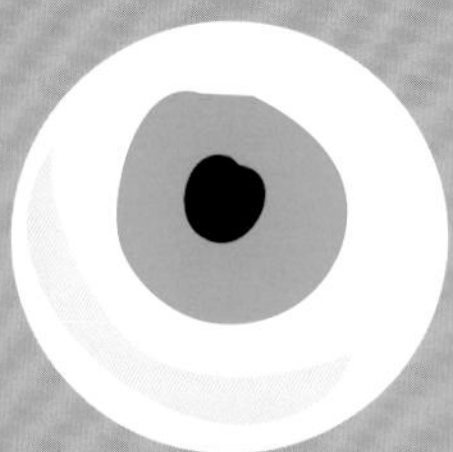

What you do

The ingredients in this recipe will make one 155 lb. (70 kg) human being. Adjust the amounts to make heavyweight boxers or lightweight ballerinas. In addition to the elements, you will need 206 bone molds and one unique human mold.

Step 1 Start with about 35 lb. (16 kg) of carbon. Warm the carbon gently and add oxygen, hydrogen, nitrogen, and sulfur to make up the organic molecules that will form the bulk of your human. (Save some oxygen to mix with calcium and phosphorus for making the bones.)

If you cannot find hydrogen and oxygen, you can simply use water instead!

Step 2 Take the phosphorus and the remaining oxygen and mix together to produce phosphate ions (PO_4^{3-}). Add the calcium and bake in the bone molds until hard.

Step 3 Take the organic molecules from step 1 and the bones from step 2 and add them to the unique human mold. At this point, add the remainder of the essential and trace elements. Since the trace elements need to be added in VERY small quantities of ppm and ppb, it is a good idea to buy a small shaker of mixed elements that can be found in the spice rack of most supermarkets. You'll have to judge these amounts by eye, since most kitchen scales cannot measure ppm or ppb!

ppm and ppb stand for "parts per million" and "parts per billion" respectively and are the equivalent of 1 in 1,000,000 and 1 in 1,000,000,000.

What's it made of?

oxygen, carbon, hydrogen, nitrogen, calcium, phosphorus, potassium, sulfur, sodium, chlorine, magnesium, iron, flourine, zinc, silicon—and 44 more elements, including gold

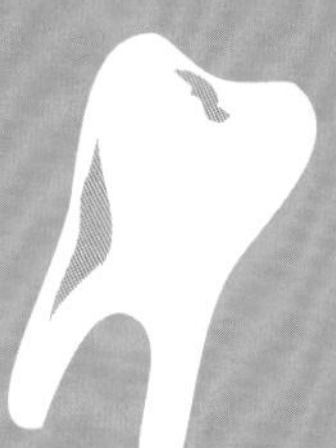

Water way to go

Did you know that you're mostly made up of water? H_2O is by far the biggest ingredient of the body. It makes up up to 60 percent of your weight. That must be where all that sweat and pee comes from!

FRANKLY speaking!

The most famous attempt to make a new human being was by Doctor Frankenstein. He was a character in a novel written about 200 years ago. But he cheated: he stuck together bits of old bodies. Then he used electricity to BLAST his creature into life. However, the creature didn't like the way it had turned out, and it started KILLING people! That's one reason to be extra careful to make sure your human turns out just right.

Step 4 Keep the raw human warm and nourished for approximately nine months (a dark place is best). When the human is fully formed, BREAK the mold to release the carbon-based life form!

You may need some adult help with this!

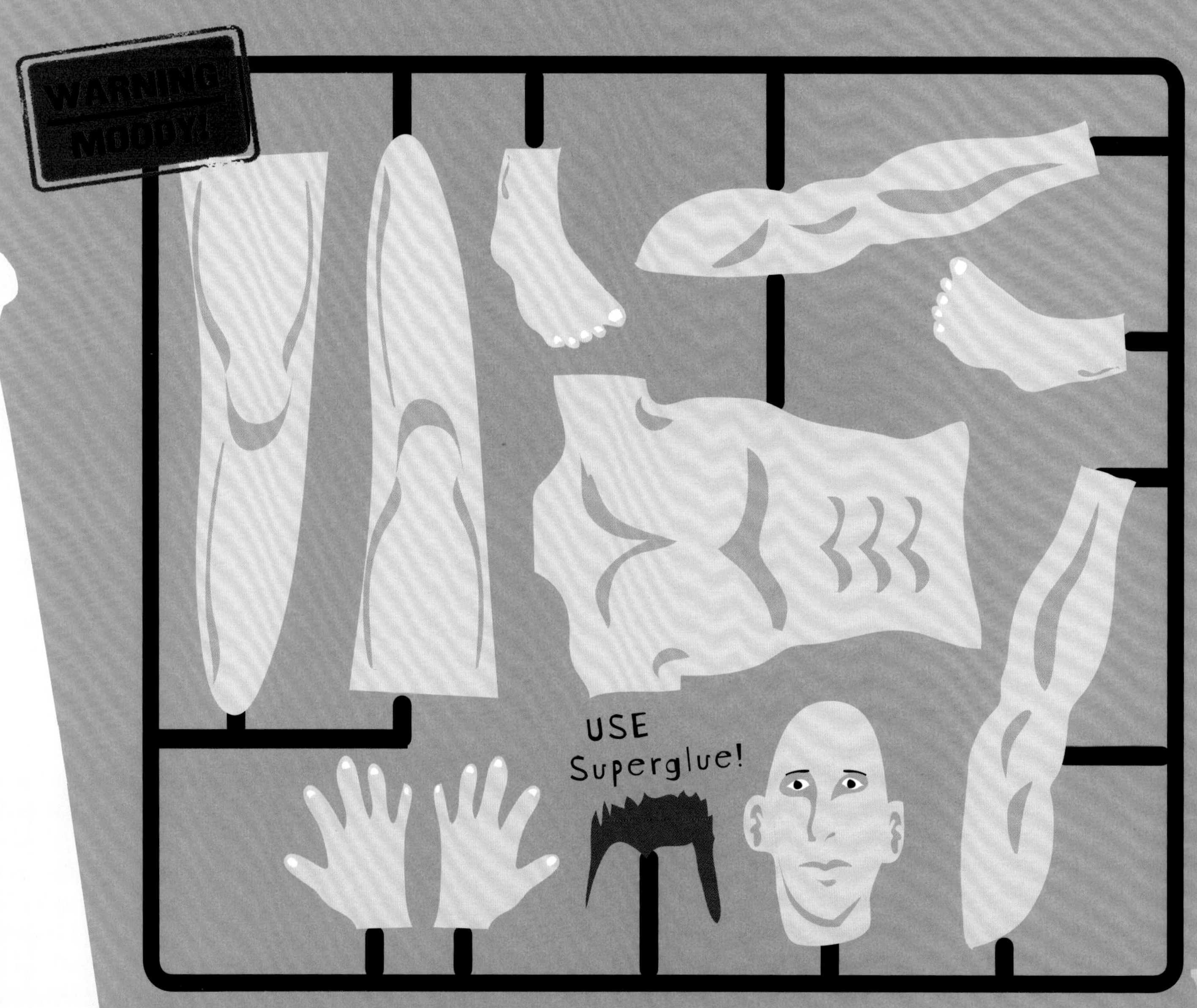
WARNING MOODY!
USE Superglue!

TREE-MENDOUS

A botanist (who studies plants) will tell you there are lots of different trees. But chemists know that they're all pretty similar underneath.

"Poly" means "many" and "saccharide" means "sugar." In a polymer, the individual units are joined together.

Whatever the type of tree, most of it is made of cellulose, a polysaccharide polymer. The cellulose only has three ingredients: carbon, hydrogen, and oxygen. It is created by linking together a bunch of sugar molecules. Most of the rest of the tree is made from lignin, which acts as a kind of glue to hold the cellulose together. Lignin is another combination of carbon, hydrogen, and oxygen. That seems simple. But trees use their basic ingredients for a few special tricks, like turning sunlight into food.

Phylling up with phuel

Chlorophyll is the chemical that makes leaves green. It also enables leaves to turn the sunlight that plants absorb into energy for them to live, in a process called photosynthesis. Chlorophyll contains magnesium, carbon, hydrogen, oxygen, and nitrogen.

WHAT'S IT MADE OF?

magnesium, carbon hydrogen, oxygen, nitrogen

WOOD YOU BELIEVE IT?

Each year a tree grows, the new wood forms a ring in the trunk. Counting the rings reveals the age of the tree. Of course, this dating method only works for trees that are no longer standing. For living trees, look at the height—and guess!

This is how to make a tree: Plant an acorn, a pine cone, or another tree seed. Water it well. Then wait for between a few years and a century for your tree to reach maturity!

TREES and the AIR

If you put a tree with a few hundred others, or a few thousand, or a few hundred thousand, what you end up with may look like a forest (because it IS a forest). But it's also a lung. Forests breathe: billions of leaves absorb CO_2 from the air and convert it into O_2. Because humans can't breathe CO_2 but love to breathe O_2, people NEED trees.

Photosynthesis

In photosynthesis, plant leaves convert carbon dioxide and water into the sugars the plant needs to survive. The chemical equation for photosynthesis is this:

Energy (in the form of light) + $6CO_2 + 6H_2O$
$\rightarrow C_6H_{12}O_6 + 6O_2$

The reaction reduces the amount of CO_2 in the air, which we can't breathe, and produces O_2, which we can. Which makes plants and trees pretty useful!

WARNING
AVOID LIGHTNING!

Veins in leaves carry energy into the plant as sugars, and carry water and minerals from the plant to the leaf.

WATER WATER EVERYWHERE

Water is pretty simple, but it's also pretty amazing. Without water, all life would cease. That makes it important stuff in anyone's book.

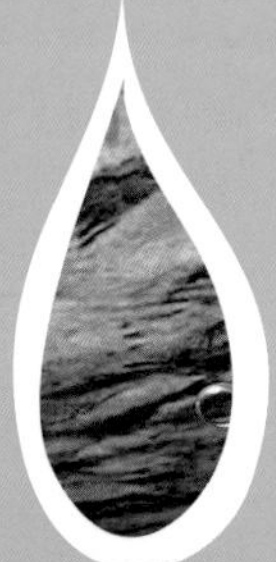

For such a simple molecule—two hydrogen atoms attached to an oxygen atom—water is an astonishing substance. Everyone knows the chemical formula of water is H_2O, but do you know its shape? The atoms are not lined up in a straight line like this: H–O–H. Instead, the hydrogens are set at an angle:

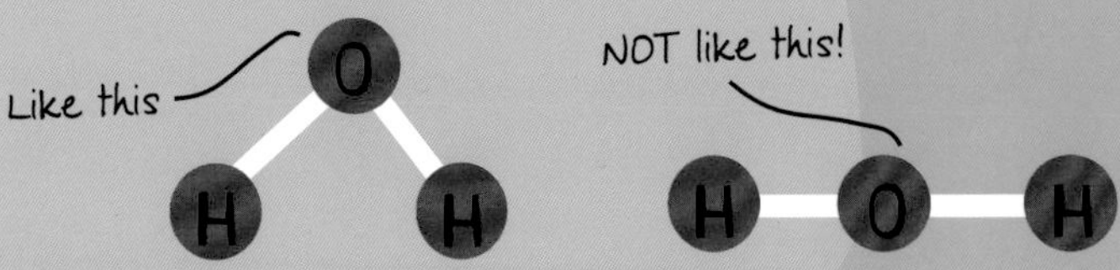

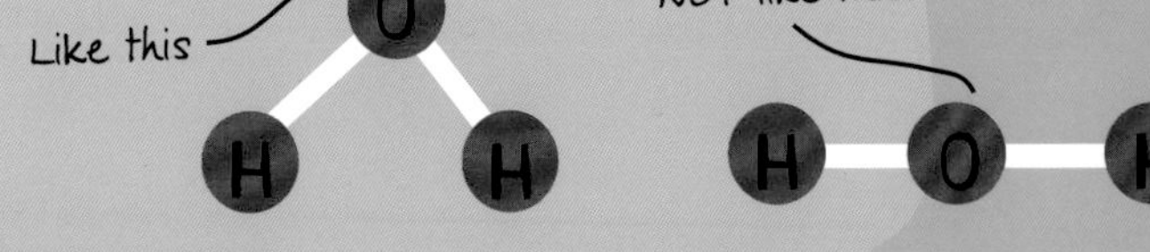

Solve it with solvents

The "bent" shape of the water molecule means that the molecule has tiny electrical charges. These charges are attracted to solids that also have electrical charges, so the water molecules surround the solids and dissolve them. Water is sometimes called the universal solvent because it dissolves so many substances. But there are also things that will NOT dissolve in water, such as OIL. A solid (or liquid) that has no electrical charges is not attracted to the water molecules, so does not dissolve. Because charged (or "polar") water dissolves charged ("polar") things, we sometimes say "like dissolves like."

Water is so good at dissolving dirt that it is used to wash everything, from your car to your teeth.

WHAT'S IT MADE OF?

hydrogen, oxygen

Not a drop to drink

The human body is about 60 percent water. We need to maintain that level to survive. Because 70 percent of the Earth's surface is covered in water, it might seem quite easy to stay alive. But if humans drink seawater, it can kill them. The salts dissolved in seawater would build up in the body and dehydrate cells and cause the kidneys to malfunction. The Dead Sea contains about nine times as much salt as regular seawater. That makes the water so dense that a person can easily float in it without swimming!

There's lots more about salts in the oceans on pages 32–33.

DRIP!

BRAIN BOX

A SWEDE BORN TO SUCCEED

Jöns Jacob Berzelius (1779–1848)

"J.J." Berzelius was a Swedish super-scientist who formulated the law of constant proportions. His law showed that any compound is always made up of the same number of atoms; for example, water is always H_2O. He also pioneered the use of chemical symbols. And J.J. discovered silicon, selenium, thorium, and cerium! In addition, his students are credited with discovering lithium and vanadium. Not a bad record, given Scandinavia was seen as a bit of a scientific backwater!

What's Your POISON?

Being bitten or stung isn't much fun. But did you know that some of the chemicals in poisons are already inside your body? It's what form they take and how much there is that really matter.

"Neuro" or "hemo"?

Snake, spider, and other venom is a complex mixture of chemicals. It varies from one species to another and can change with the climate, where the animal lives, and even its age. All venoms work in one of two ways. They attack either by paralyzing the victim and damaging the respiratory system (perhaps by a heart attack) or by affecting the bloodstream (perhaps by preventing blood clots and causing severe bleeding). The first type are called neurotoxins; the second type are hemotoxins. Most venoms contain lots of organic molecules (carbon-based molecules with hydrogen, nitrogen, oxygen, and other atoms attached). Some of the most important molecules are proteins and enzymes. These compounds can cause the breakdown of human tissue and lead to massive bleeding and organ failure.

The respiratory system controls breathing, which gets oxygen into the bloodstream.

WATCH OUT!

WHAT'S IT MADE OF?

carbon, hydrogen, oxygen, nitrogen

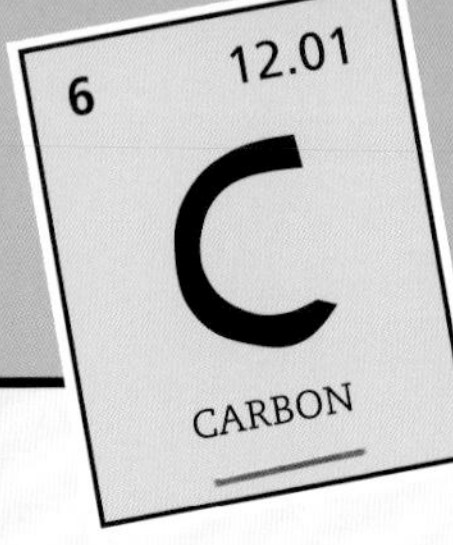

Elementary stuff

Carbon

- **Atomic Number: 6**
- Atomic Mass: 12.01
- **Isotopes: 2 naturally occurring isotopes**
- Boiling Point: 7,281˚F (4,027˚C) (sublimes—goes straight from solid to gas)
- **Melting Point (diamond): 6,400˚F (3,500˚C)**

Carbon is arguably THE most important element. It forms the basis for all organic molecules, which are the building blocks of all life forms. Carbon loves itself, and C atoms bond into huge and complicated molecules. The best known is DNA (or **D**eoxyribo**N**ucleic **A**cid), the blueprint for all life. Carbon atoms also form most of the molecules that we eat, like sugars, fats, proteins, and fiber.

It's not all doom and gloom

Some venom can be useful. It is used in the production of anti-venom and also in medical research for such diseases as Parkinson's and Alzheimer's. Some snake venom has been used in situations where blood clots are dangerous. It thins the blood, which is helpful as long as it's controlled. The cone snail defends itself with a poisonous harpoon: the venom from it has been developed into a powerful painkiller. Doctors also believe that venom from the copperhead snake might be the basis of an anti-cancer drug.

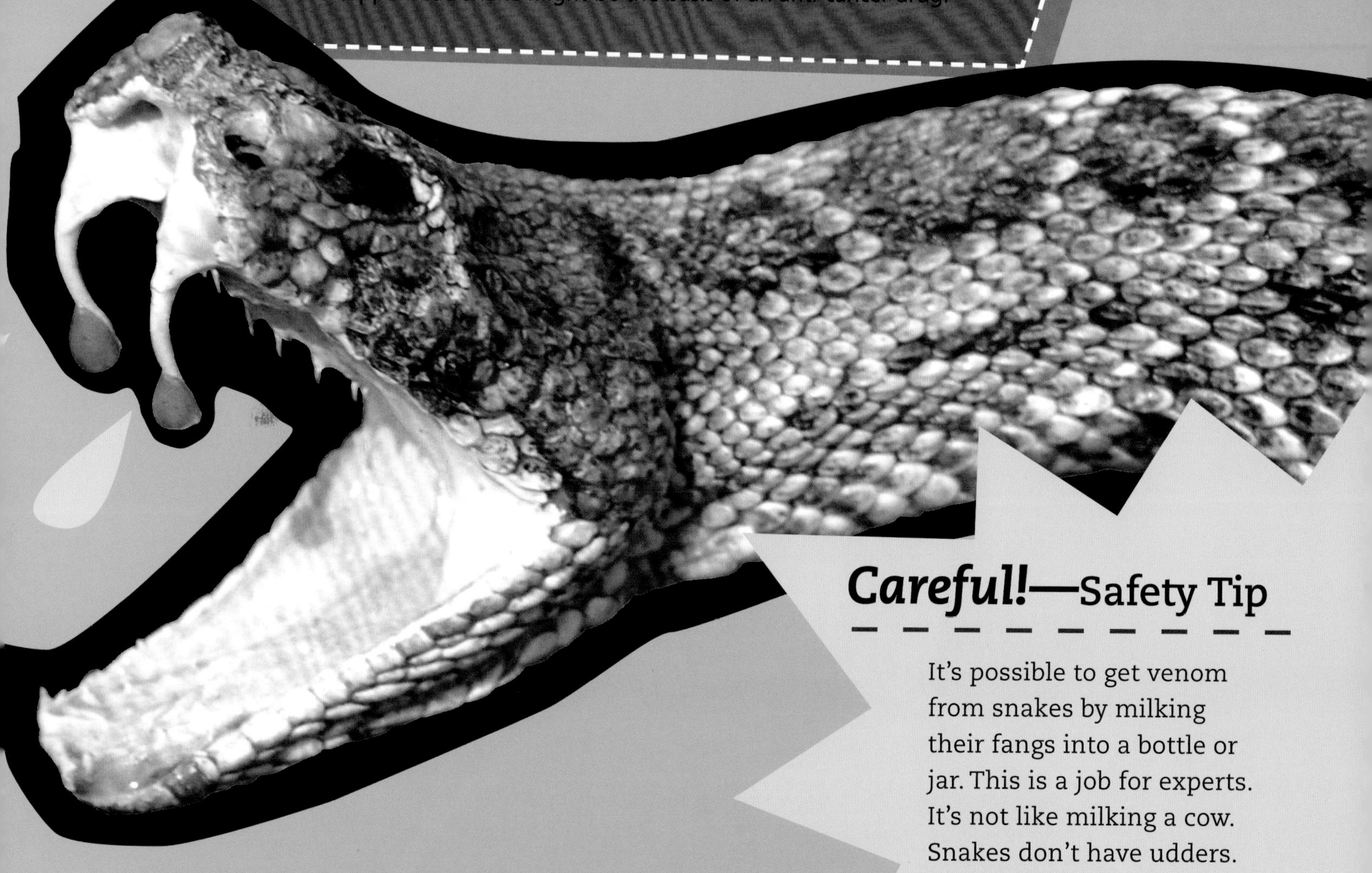

ANTIDOTE

Careful!—Safety Tip

It's possible to get venom from snakes by milking their fangs into a bottle or jar. This is a job for experts. It's not like milking a cow. Snakes don't have udders. And they're too low to fit a milking stool underneath.

What a shocker!

The venom from an insect sting or bite can cause other problems. If the victim has an allergic reaction to the bite, he or she can go into what's called an "anaphylactic shock." The venom causes the body to release huge amounts of natural biochemicals that cause airways to become restricted, hives on the skin, heart palpitations, sweating, and mental confusion. This is not caused by the venom, but by an allergic reaction to the toxin. But it's still just as life-threatening!

Biochemicals are natural, but can still be dangerous in large quantities.

He
MOO!
H
Ti
Te
Sb
Cf
Strike a MATCH!
OK, who pulled the string?
Ra
Xe
WARNING BRIGHT!
Ho
Fe

DAILY LIFE

Everything you touch, everything you can see, everything you eat and drink: elements are everywhere. But how does an element know whether it's supposed to be part of food or part of a car?

ILLUMINATION!

A light bulb needs just three parts. The tricky bit is to get something hot enough to glow...without bursting into flames!

WHAT'S IT MADE OF?

tungsten, argon, silicon, oxygen, mercury, bromine, iodine

1. A FILAMENT: The glowing part of the bulb is made of 2 $1/2$ ft. (2 m) of very thin tungsten wire wound into a double coil.

2. INERT GAS: When it is hot enough to glow, the tungsten filament could react with oxygen in the air and combust. So, to prevent the tungsten from bursting into flames, the oxygen around the filament is replaced with an inert gas—one possibility is argon.

The inert gases got their name because they don't react with many other elements.

3. A GLASS BULB: This stops the gas from escaping. The filament and the inert gas are put inside a thin glass bulb made from silicon, oxygen, and some other elements like mercury, bromine, and iodine. Most bulbs are made of transparent glass, but opaque or colored glass works, too.

Elementary stuff

Tungsten

- **Atomic Number: 74**
- Atomic Mass: 183.85
- **Isotopes: 5 natural isotopes**
- Boiling Point: 10,031˚F (5,555˚C)
- **Melting Point: 6,192˚F (3,422˚C)**

Don't be misled by tungsten's chemical symbol into thinking that this tough element is really called "wungsten." In fact, tungsten was once known as wolfram (German for "wolf dirt") because it was extracted from the mineral wolframite. Tungsten has the highest melting point of any metal, so it's ideal for filaments. But it's also tough enough to be used for bulletproof armor plating. One of its compounds, tungsten carbide, is hard enough to make high-speed cutting tools and drill bits.

Edison was America's greatest inventor: he held well over 1,000 patents for his inventions—that's a record!

EDISON

INCANDESCENCE

Incandescence describes the tendency for materials to GLOW when heated and give off red, orange, yellow, and white light. The problem is that, as well as the light, up to 90 percent of the energy is wasted as heat—which won't help you see in the dark but does explain why a light bulb gets so hot.

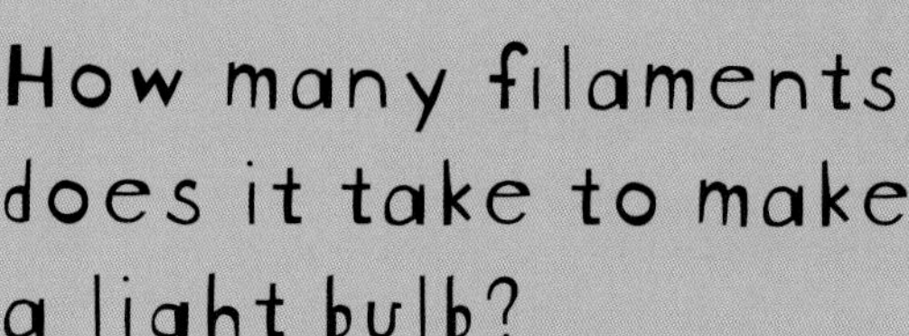

How many filaments does it take to make a light bulb?

Well, the answer for Thomas Alva Edison was LOTS! Edison experimented with hundreds, even thousands, of possible materials in the first light bulbs. The key to success was finding a material for the filament that was long lasting but also cheap. In the early 20th century, General Electric Company engineer William Coolidge found that tungsten was an excellent material for filaments because it has such a high melting point (around 6,100°F, or 3,400°C).

Filament Test Log
by T.A.Edison

~~Horsehair~~ RUBBISH!
~~platinum~~ Promising—but expensive!
~~Gold~~
~~Silver~~ TOO EXPENSIVE!
~~paper~~ Make sure it's carbonized first!
~~cotton~~ CARBONIZE!
~~bamboo~~ ?? Maybe if carbonized
tungsten ✓✓

HALOGEN BULBS use a group 17 element to react with the tungsten and redeposit atoms back on to the filament, which extends the life of the bulb.

All explained on page 9!

FLUORESCENT LIGHTS have a sealed tube containing noble gases and some mercury. Electricity excites electrons in the gas, which give off ultra-violet light. The UV light is converted to visible light when it hits the inside of the tube, which is coated with a phosphor.

Phosphors are metal compounds that glow after they have been exposed to a source of light.

NEON LIGHTS contain neon and other gases and give off colored light when their electrons are "excited."

STRIKE A MATCH!

Lighting a match is like causing a mini-explosion. The chemicals on the match have to be active enough to burst into flames, but only when you want them to. No one wants exploding pockets!

WARNING VERY HOT!!

CRACKLE!

The "safety" match was invented in 1844. It is "safe" because the ingredients that make it burst into flames are separate: some are on the match, but some are on the striking surface. That makes it harder to accidentally set yourself on fire.

Friction burn!

Chlorates are salts that combine oxygen and chlorine. They are also used to make fireworks!

The striking surface is made mainly of red phosphorus and powdered glass. The match head is mainly made of potassium chlorate ($KClO_3$) and sulfur. When the match is struck, friction ignites the phosphorus and potassium chlorate in a mini-explosion. Early matchboxes had the striking surface inside: CRAZY! When it was moved to the outside, matches got more popular—and much safer!

Important safety tip

NEVER play with matches. Safety matches might be "safe," but the flames they cause are as dangerous as any others. They're real. They can burn you or someone else, or set fire to stuff around you.

DANGER!

The first matches used white phosphorus, which ignites easily, is fiercely hot, and causes terrible burns. It also produces clouds of dense smoke. In fact, it's so dangerous and smoky that it has been used in smoke bombs and even as a chemical weapon. Not what you want for lighting candles at Christmas! And that wasn't the only problem. Workers in match factories became ill with ailments caused by the chemical, including "phossy jaw." This horrible disease caused swelling of the gums, toothaches, and rotting of the jawbone, which decayed and gave off a dreadful stench!

Red and white phosphorus are allotropes—different forms of the same pure element, just like graphite and diamond for carbon.

Are you a phillumenist?

A what?! Well, the answer's YES if you collect matchboxes and match-related items! Sounds like a weird hobby? Remember, companies used to advertise their businesses by making their own matches in special boxes, so there are many to collect. (Of course, it's safer to make sure to collect only empty matchboxes!)

WHAT'S IT MADE OF?

phosphorus, potassium, chlorine, oxygen, silicon, sulfur

Elementary stuff

16 32.07
S
SULFUR

- **Atomic Number: 16**
- Atomic Mass: 32.10
- **Isotopes: 4 naturally occurring isotopes**
- Boiling Point: 832˚F (444˚C)
- **Melting Point: 240˚F (115˚C)**

Sulfur

Sulfur is a vivid yellow, non-metal substance known to ancient peoples because it occurs in volcanic eruptions; they thought it came straight from HELL—literally! As an element, sulfur often forms rings of eight atoms joined together in the S_8 molecule. Today we associate sulfur and its compounds with bad smells like rotten eggs. Pee-yew!

How to Make Money

What's it made of?
copper, silver, gold, zinc, nickel, tin, iron, carbon

Coins were once made from valuable metals like gold, but crooks kept shaving bits off them. Today most coins are made from metals that only have symbolic value.

Dozens of different metals have been used over the centuries for making coins, but three have been used SO often and SO commonly that they have become known as the "coinage metals": copper, silver, and gold. They also happen to be the three elements in group 11 of the periodic table. Today, most countries use a mixture, or alloy, of different metals to make coins.

Alloys are mixtures of metals: bronze is a mixture of copper and tin, and steel is a mixture of iron and carbon.

Where has the copper gone?

The first U.S. penny was minted in 1783 and was 100 percent pure copper. Since then, its composition has changed many times. In 1856, it was 88 percent copper and 12 percent nickel. In 1962, it was 95 percent copper and 5 percent zinc. Today, it is 97.5 percent zinc and 2.5 percent copper—copper-plated zinc.

At times the value of copper has risen so sharply that the value of the metal in the one-cent coins was greater than the face value of the coin!

Elementary stuff

- **Atomic Number: 29**
- Atomic Mass: 63.55
- **Isotopes: 2 natural isotopes**
- Boiling Point: 5,301˚F (2,927˚C)
- **Melting Point: 1,983˚F (1,084˚C)**

Copper

Copper is a metal that ancient civilizations used to make tools and weapons. Its common modern uses are in electrical devices (as thin wires) and in construction for roofs and pipes. It is often mixed in alloys such as bronze (copper and tin) and brass (copper and zinc). Some animals, like the octopus, have a compound containing copper in their blood that helps carry oxygen around their bodies. It makes their blood blue, not red!

U.S. Quarter: copper 91.7%, nickel 8.3

TRY THIS

Cleaning COINS

Would you like some new money? Well, we can't actually make NEW coins like the U.S. Mint, but we can clean up old ones so that they LOOK like new.

WHAT YOU'LL NEED

some old, dirty pennies
salt
white vinegar

1. Put enough vinegar into a bowl to cover the pennies that you have.
2. Add a generous sprinkle of salt.
3. Drop the pennies in the bowl, spread them out, and leave them for 10 minutes.
4. Remove the pennies and let them dry on a paper towel.

How does that work? When pennies get "dirty" they are actually reacting with the oxygen in the air to form a layer of dull copper oxide on the outer surface of the coin. The combination of the acidic vinegar (which is actually ethanoic acid) and the salt (sodium chloride) helps to dissolve this outer oxide layer and reveal the shiny copper metal underneath. As good as new...

What about "silver" coins?

Nah...they're not silver either. Usually they are made of a copper and nickel alloy called cupro-nickel. The U.S. nickel is 75 percent copper and 25 percent nickel. The dime, quarter and half dollar are all 91.7 percent copper and 8.3 percent nickel.

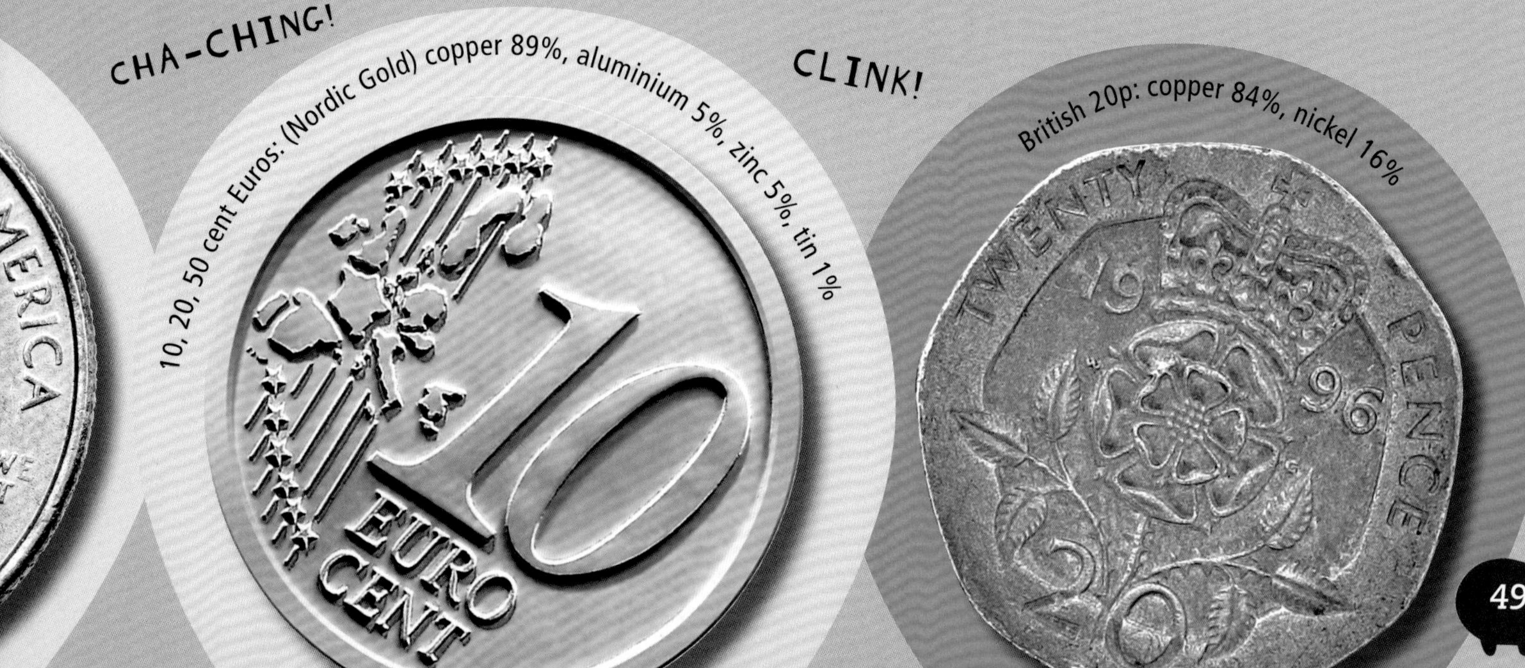

The Chemistry of FIZZ-ICS

Everyone loves fizzy drinks. In fact, they're really nothing more than water and carbon dioxide (apart from the flavorings and the sugar…lots and lots of sugar).

The problem is that colorless, odorless, tasteless water with colorless, odorless, tasteless CO_2 dissolved in it isn't something that most people actually want to drink. So most fizzy drinks have large amounts of sugars, colorings, flavorings, and preservatives added.

Sugars are carbohydrates made mainly from carbon, oxygen, and hydrogen.

All "fizzy" drinks are "carbonated"—they have carbon dioxide gas dissolved in them to create bubbles. The gas is forced into the water with a large amount of pressure and the bottle is sealed. When the bottle is opened, the pressure is released and the gas comes bubbling out of the liquid, causing the FIZZZZZZZ sound. When a fizzy drink warms up, the carbon dioxide escapes from the water. That's why fizzy drinks go "flat." Our bodies are carbon-dioxide factories. When we breathe we take in oxygen and then convert it to waste, CO_2. It's the main gas we breathe out.

BRAIN BOX

BY GUM, IT'S OXYGEN!

Joseph Priestley (1733–1804)

Englishman Priestley was one crazy scientist. Not only was he involved in experiments with electricity and chemistry, but he also studied several nonscientific subjects, including work on English grammar, theology, and metaphysics. He is most famous for generally being credited with the discovery of what he called "dephlogisticated air," or oxygen, in 1774. Less well known, but more delicious, is his invention of soda water—fizzy drinks!

WHAT'S IT **MADE OF?**

hydrogen, oxygen, carbon

FIZZZZZ!

THE REAL THING

Fizzy drinks are known as "sodas" after Priestley's invention, "soda water." Without doubt, the most famous fizzy drink in the world was invented in the United States at the end of the 19th century. Coca-Cola was originally sold at drug stores, which had soda fountains installed because carbonated water was supposed to have health benefits. Coca-Cola has since become known around the world. Its ingredients are a closely guarded secret: apart from water, carbon dioxide, and sugar!

Dentists' enemy number ONE

SWEET!

What's the worst thing for your teeth? Sugar, right? Wrong! Even worse is sugar dissolved in acid, which means most fizzy drinks. When carbon dioxide dissolves in water, it forms a weak solution of carbonic acid. The acid makes fizzy drinks corrosive. It can eat away at tooth enamel, causing decay. The combination of acid and high levels of sugar make fizzy drinks a dentist's nightmare. (Unless, of course, a dentist fancies a cold drink on a summer day!)

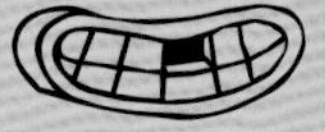

FAST FOOD!

Food is all about organic chemistry. That doesn't mean organic as in organic farming. In chemistry, "organic" refers to chemicals that are made mainly from carbon atoms.

Carbon is pretty cool because it can form bonds with itself as well as with other elements. This means that carbon can form chains, rings, and cages of almost any length and shape. It can also combine with many other elements to produce a virtually never-ending number of compounds. All life forms are made up of organic compounds of one sort or another.

The bun is mainly starches and sugars.

Mmmm...triglycerides

Vegetable oils and animal fats are the main components of all kinds of fast food, including burgers and fries. Most of these oils and fats are made from organic compounds called triglycerides. A triglyceride is a compound made from glycerol (an alcohol with the chemical formula $C_3H_8O_3$) and one of a number of other chemicals called "fatty acids." The fatty acids are also organic compounds. They have long chains of carbon atoms with lots of hydrogen atoms hanging off them.

Fatty acids are good sources of energy because they're hydrophobic: they don't like water molecules, which take up room in foods like carbohydrates.

What fat's that?

Fatty acids can be either saturated or unsaturated. If the fatty acid has carbon atoms that are bonded together in a chain with at least one double bond—a bond in which two atoms share two pairs of electrons—then the fat is called unsaturated. In saturated fats, carbon atoms are joined together in the chain with single bonds. Some saturated fats are popular with fast-food manufacturers since they help to prolong the shelf life of food and stop it from going rotten. BUT they are linked to health problems, so try not to eat too many.

You may also have heard of "trans fats." This phrase describes different kinds of unsaturated fats, depending on the shape of the organic molecule. So are they better for you than saturated fats? The answer is NO! You should try to avoid eating too many of those as well!

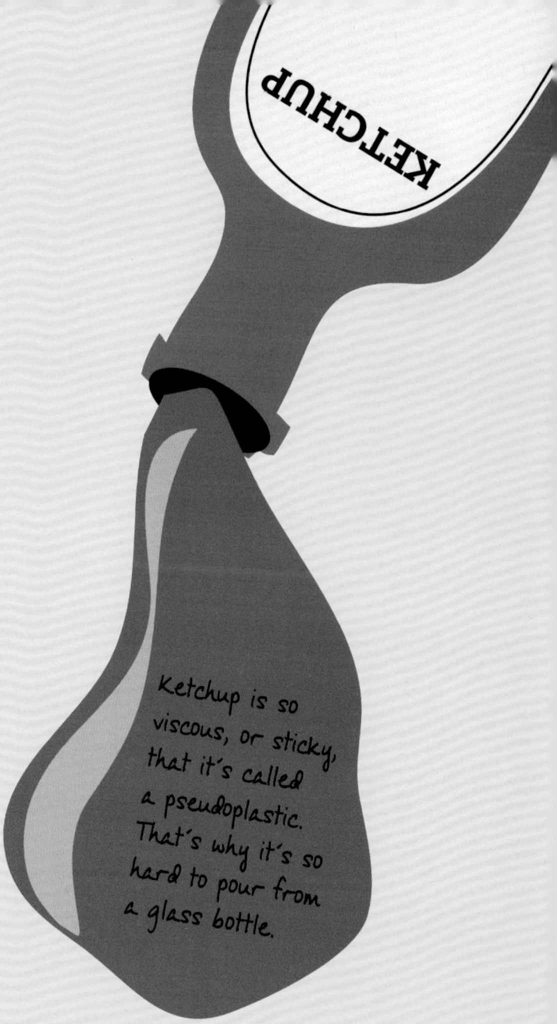

KETCHUP

Ketchup is so viscous, or sticky, that it's called a pseudoplastic. That's why it's so hard to pour from a glass bottle.

Mmmmm...

WHAT'S IT MADE OF?

carbon, hydrogen, nitrogen, sulfur, oxygen

PROTEINS

The beef in a burger, like all muscles and other parts of animals, is made up of proteins. Proteins are organic, so they are made mainly from carbon atoms. They have hydrogen, oxygen, nitrogen, and other atoms added. Proteins are chains of yet another class of organic compounds called amino acids. Unlike lots of fats and oils, proteins ARE good for us. In a normal diet, proteins are important since they help build and repair muscle and tissue, make the blood work properly, and help with all kinds of other functions of your body.

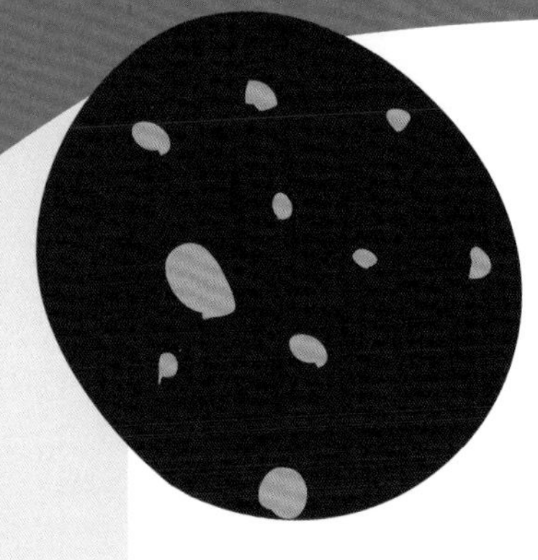

A Bedtime SNACK

How would you like to be offered a dish of hydrogen, oxygen, nitrogen, and calcium? Or how about carbohydrates, fats, and amino acids? They're both the same to you and me: milk and cookies!

Sweet carbs

Milk is close to 90 percent water—good old H_2O—but the next largest ingredient is sugar. About 5 percent of regular cows' milk is a carbohydrate called lactose. That's why lactose is sometimes called "milk sugar." Carbohydrates are molecules that are made of carbon, hydrogen, and oxygen atoms. Lactose is a disaccharide: "di" means "two" and "saccharide" means "sugar," so it's a molecule made of two sugars joined together. The sugars that make up lactose are glucose and galactose.

Carbohydrates are the most common source of energy for living things.

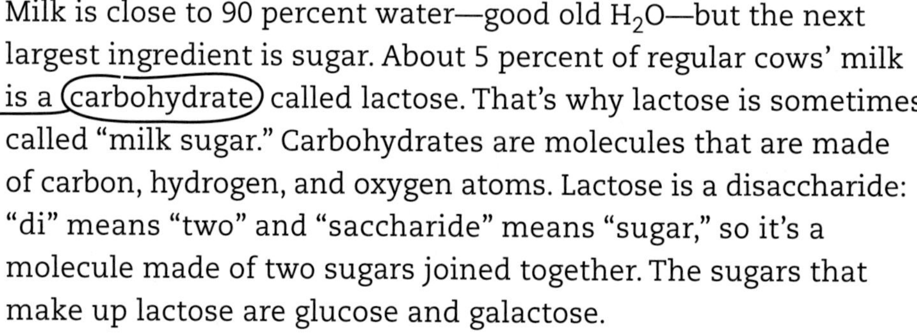

Fat formula

Milk contains about 3 to 4 percent fat. Fats are large organic molecules. In chemistry, the word "organic" refers to molecules that are composed mainly of carbon atoms with other atoms attached. A typical fat found in milk can have well over 100 atoms with hydrogen and oxygen atoms attached to long chains of carbon atoms.

Amino acids and proteins

Amino acids are organic molecules that are necessary for the human body to function correctly. Some are classed as "essential," meaning that the body needs them but cannot make them. Instead, they must be obtained from food. There are 22 amino acids in total. When mixtures of these molecules join together to form long chains, they are called proteins. Milk contains about 3 to 4 percent protein.

WHAT'S IT MADE OF?

carbon, hydrogen, oxygen, nitrogen, and some calcium

COOKIE jar

What's in a cookie? Well, it's complicated, but basically it's all organic stuff. Flour is essentially starch, and there's lots of sugar—both organic molecules. If you want chocolate chips, then you'll have to add more sugar, fats, a few vitamins and minerals, and maybe even some caffeine (which is another organic molecule that also occurs in coffee).

Liquid energy

Milk is a great source of energy because it contains lots of fats and minerals, but it's also REALLY easy to digest. That's why mammals feed it to their young, whose digestive systems are not fully developed.

REALLY COOL SCIENCE BIT

Alphabet soup? I thought it was milk!

Milk contains a whole bunch of vitamins including A, B_1, B_2, B_3, B_5, B_6, B_{12}, C, D, and E. Vitamins are some crazy organic molecules that provide essential materials to the body. They are formed by many carbon atoms joined together in weird and wonderful rings and chains, with even more hydrogen, oxygen, nitrogen, and other atoms attached. You'll also find a bunch of other elements in milk that are useful to the body. The most important ones are calcium, magnesium, phosphorus, potassium, selenium, and zinc. You might have seen milk advertised as an important source of calcium. It is, but there is only a very tiny amount of calcium in a whole glass. That's probably NOT as much as you thought! (It's lucky that the body doesn't need very much.)

CRACKLE!

SNAP!

Crystal clear!
Pm
BOOM!
Te
Sb
Diamonds
are
FOREVER
Xe
WARNING
EXPENSIVE!
C
Fe

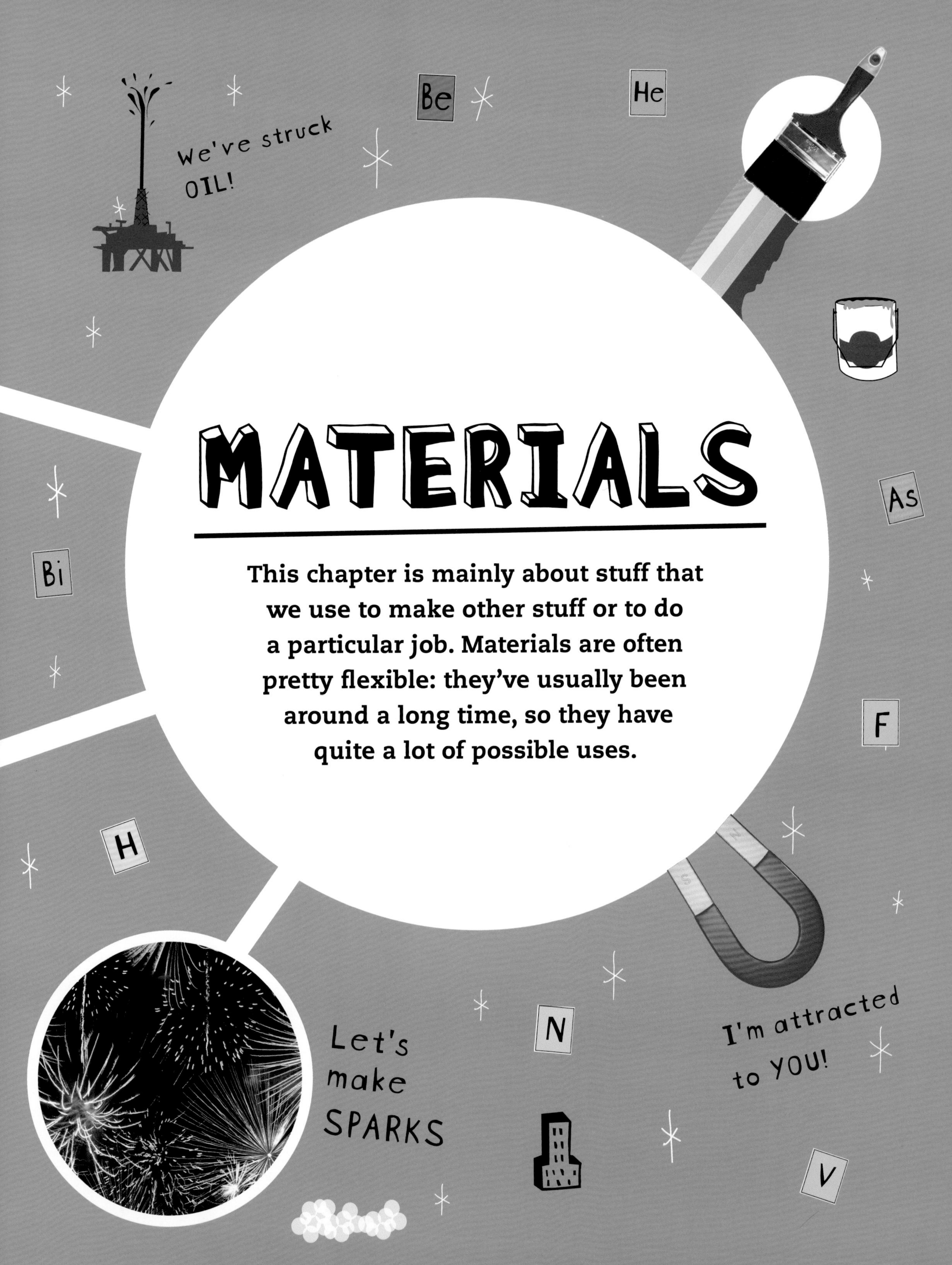

MATERIALS

This chapter is mainly about stuff that we use to make other stuff or to do a particular job. Materials are often pretty flexible: they've usually been around a long time, so they have quite a lot of possible uses.

Whoosh!

FUN WITH FIREWORKS!

WOW!

Ever wondered how fireworks work? With elements and chemical compounds, that's how. They're packed into a tube and made so hot they glow different colors.

Step 1 Start with fuel for burning: Carbon works well, in the form of charcoal. Carbon also comes in the form of diamonds, but they don't burn quite as well. They also make your fireworks too expensive! Sulfur can also be used as a fuel, but it will make your fireworks STINK! You have been warned!

WARNING
OXIDIZERS ARE EXPLOSIVE!

Step 2 Add an oxidizer to make the fuel burn: these chemicals produce the oxygen atoms that allow the fuels to burn or combust. Good things to use as oxidizers are chlorates and perchlorates (ions that include chlorine and oxygen), or nitrates made from nitrogen and oxygen.

Step 3 Use some binder to hold your firework ingredients together. Dextrin (a compound made of C, H and O atoms) can be used as a kind of firework glue.

Different forms of the same element are called "allotropes."

Important safety tip

Fireworks contain a lot of carbon in the black powder that shoots the firework into the sky. Human beings also contain a lot of carbon. Don't get mixed up and try to shoot Granny into the sky. It WON'T work.

For Smoke
Add zinc
For Sparks
Add iron
WARNING
NO MATCHES OR SPARKS
DANGER!
An ancient Chinese cook mixed charcoal, sulfur, and saltpeter... and got the first firework.
STAND BACK! When sulfur burns, it releases sulfur dioxide— which is poisonous!
BEWARE! CONTAINS EXPLODING POWDER
(For people who don't speak science... that means FIREWORKS!)
MIXED WITH: aluminum, antimony, barium, calcium, copper, iron, lithium, magnesium, sodium, strontium, titanium, or zinc
WHAT'S IT MADE OF?
carbon, sulfur, oxygen, phosphorus, chlorine, potassium
For Red
Add lithium, or lithium carbonate, or strontium
For Yellow
Add sodium and sodium compounds such as cryolite
For Green
Add barium
For Blue
Add copper and copper compounds
For Orange
Add salts of calcium
For White and Silver
Add flakes of aluminium, magnesium, or titanium— all of which get white hot

Really COOL Science Bit

Many elements make light work

Incandescence describes light produced by heat. You can make firework fuel glow red, orange, yellow, or white depending on the temperature. For greens and blues, you have to add other chemicals and rely on **luminescence**. You can also make red, orange, yellow, and white that way. Luminescence is light that is given off when electrons in chemicals move around. The color depends upon the elements that you add—the firework on the left tells you how.

Incandescence Luminescence

BA-BA-BOOM!

An explosion is a normal chemical reaction—but it happens very, very fast. That means that it brings lots of heat and energy along for the ride.

Thinking in reverse

Many explosives contain nitrogen. You probably already know that nitrogen gas makes up about 78 percent of the air around us, so why isn't ordinary air explosive? To find out, you have to think in reverse. It might be a surprise to learn that explosions aren't caused by things blowing apart, but by things coming together!

The nature of nitrogen

The nitrogen in air is a molecule that bonds together a pair of atoms, N_2. The two atoms are bonded together with a mega-strong force. That means that it takes a HUGE amount of energy to split them apart, so the nitrogen gas is very stable or inert.

An inert element is something that doesn't react with other elements.

SSSS...

Alfie invents dynamite!

Swedish rich guy and chemist Alfred Nobel (who also started the institute that gives out the Nobel prizes) invented dynamite in 1867. He took nitroglycerine ($C_3H_5N_3O_9$—another compound containing nitrogen) and mixed it with a powdery rock called kieselguhr. Without the rock, nitroglycerine was way too dangerous. It was so unstable a jolt could make it explode. Nobel already knew that: in 1864 an explosion at his factory killed several workers, including his brother Emil.

WHAM!

Really COOL Science Bit

What about 2,4,6-trinitrotoluene?

What sort of a CRAZY name is that? To be honest, most people just call it TNT! That "N" tells you that there's more nitrogen involved. This time it's tied up inside a yellow solid. TNT is a useful explosive because it doesn't explode on impact, it's water resistant, and it can be melted into a liquid and poured where it is needed. You think TNT has a complicated chemical name? How about two other common explosives: HMX (cyclotetramethylenetetranitramine) and RDX (cyclotrimethylenetrinitramine)?

WHAT'S IT MADE OF?

nitrogen, hydrogen, carbon, oxygen, sodium

WARNING VERY HOT!!

The energy is released in the form of heat that spreads out in an expanding wave. There's quite a lot of noise, too!

If a chemical explosive contains lots of separate nitrogen atoms, the atoms react by coming together to make N_2. Making bonds between atoms is the opposite of breaking them. So instead of energy being used to split the molecule apart, the creation of the bond RELEASES energy. And because it's a mega-strong bond, it releases a huge amount of energy. That's why explosions go BANG!

Explosives for SAFETY?

Would you believe that some explosives are actually useful BECAUSE they blow up so easily. Take azides. They're really dangerous to handle, but sodium azide (NaN_3) is used in car airbags BECAUSE it is so reactive! If there is a collision, the sodium azide's nitrogen atoms almost instantly rearrange themselves to form nitrogen gas (N_2). The gas blows up the car's airbag in a fraction of a second.

BOOM!

Puttering Around with PAINTS!

Watching paint dry is supposed to be one of the most BORING things in the world. As any chemist will tell you, though, that paint is far more fascinating than you might think!

Phased by colloids?

Many paints are colloids. A colloid is a substance that has one phase (a solid, liquid, or gas) finely dispersed in another phase (another solid, liquid, or gas). The dispersed phase is called the dispersed phase (imagine that!). The other phase is called the continuous phase. In paint, the continuous phase is often water and the dispersed phase is often an organic molecule like urethane. The particles of a colloid (the dispersed phase) are very, very, very, very tiny. Or maybe even TINIER. They are bigger than molecules, but you can't see them through a microscope. One type of colloid is an emulsion. In an emulsion, both the dispersed phase and the continuous phase are liquids. Latex of water-based paint is an emulsion.

An organic molecule is one made of carbon.

PAINT
WHAT'S IT MADE OF?
hydrogen,
oxygen,
carbon,
titanium

SPLOSH!

A pigment absorbs light of certain wavelengths and only reflects light of other wavelengths, which is what creates color.

What about color?

For most people, the most important thing about paint is its color. The colors come from pigment. Perhaps the pigment most commonly used is titanium dioxide. It is responsible for the bright white color of white paint. It also makes the paint opaque, so you cannot see through it. Other pigments, both natural and artificial, give other colors to paint.

It's like watching paint dry!

You've probably heard that phrase used to describe something very boring. But would you believe that, when paint dries, it's actually really cool? As the continuous phase (the water) evaporates, billions of the dispersed phase particles join together to make a polymer (poly means "many"). They form a thin, solid layer—that's the paint on the wall. You may know the word "polyurethane." That's the "many" urethane molecules coming together to make a coating.

Common COLLOIDS at home

You may not realize, but you already know lots of colloids in common household items.
TOOTHPASTE = a solid dispersed in a liquid, which is a colloid called a SOL
MANY SPRAYS = a liquid dispersed in a gas, which is a colloid called an AEROSOL
MAYONNAISE = a liquid dispersed in a liquid, which is a colloid called an EMULSION
SHAVING CREAM = a gas dispersed in a liquid, which is a colloid called a FOAM

DAZZLING WITH DIAMONDS

It's amazing what a single element can do—if it's the right element. Step forward carbon. With a lot of pressure and a long time, carbon turns into stones that sparkle like glass.

While some people might think chemistry is the "hardest" subject, everyone agrees that diamond is the hardest known naturally occurring substance. And to make a diamond you only need ONE element! Yep, that's it: one lonely, boring old element—element number 6, carbon.

Industry uses loads of diamonds in tools because they're so hard they'll cut through ANYTHING.

S-L-O-W pressure

Diamonds may be a girl's best friend (according to the old song), so it's lucky that they come ready-made. No fashionista or bride-to-be would be impressed with the pile of rocks that diamonds are made from—or the time they would have to wait. Naturally occurring diamonds are formed by MASSIVE temperatures and pressures acting upon carbon-containing minerals deep in the Earth's crust. These transformations take place over billions of years. Volcanic eruptions bring the stones closer to the surface of the Earth, where they can be mined. South and central Africa are rich sources for diamond mines, but diamonds can be found in many parts of the world.

Diamonds can be made in labs. They're okay for industry, but not to wear—not if you want to look good, anyway!

Diamonds are formed over 60 mi. (100 km) deep in the Earth's crust.

It's super-hot down there, and subject to HUGE pressure.

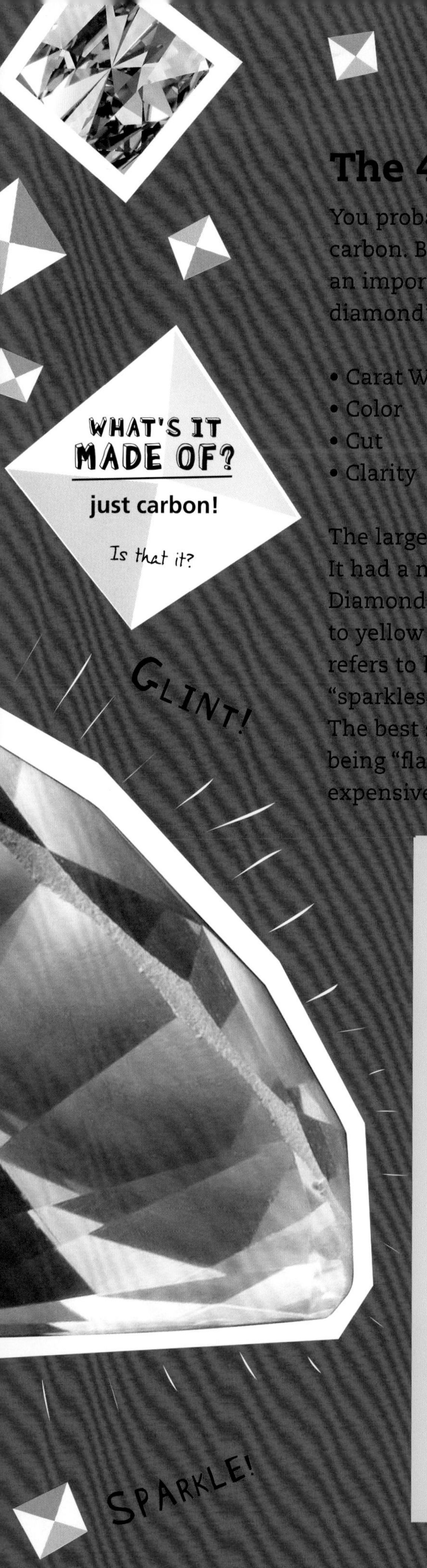

WHAT'S IT MADE OF?
just carbon!
Is that it?
GLINT!
SPARKLE!

The 4 Cs

You probably know that C is the chemical symbol for carbon. But did you know that the letter "C" also plays an important role in how diamonds are classified? A diamond's quality is measured by the "4 Cs":

- Carat Weight (1 carat = 0.007 oz. or 200 mg)
- Color
- Cut
- Clarity

The largest diamond ever found is the Cullinan Diamond. It had a mass of about 1.4 lb. (621 g)—over 3,100 carats! Diamonds can take on many colors, ranging from brown to yellow to white (white is best). The "cut" of diamond refers to how well it reflects light, and therefore how well it "sparkles." "Clarity" refers to any BLEMISHES or inclusions. The best stones have no inclusions and are described as being "flawless"—these are VERY rare and therefore VERY expensive (for something that comes out of the ground).

Not this kind of carrot!!

Really COOL Science Bit

Carbon copies

Diamond is only one of carbon's different forms. Another common form of pure carbon is graphite—the "lead" in your pencil. But graphite is very soft and diamond is as hard as…diamond. Why the difference? IT'S ALL IN THE STRUCTURE. Whether you get graphite or diamond depends upon how the carbon atoms bond together. At very high temperatures, diamonds can even be converted to graphite. Other forms of pure carbon are called fullerenes, the best known of these are the 3-D formations called "buckyballs" and "buckytubes." The first fullerene discovered was named buckminsterfullerene after Richard Buckminster Fuller because the shape of the molecule resembled his famous geodesic domes.

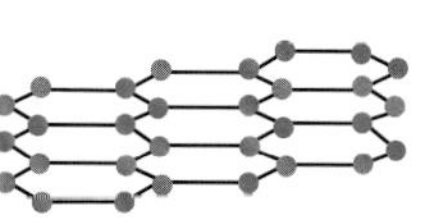

Graphite (C)

Diamond (C)

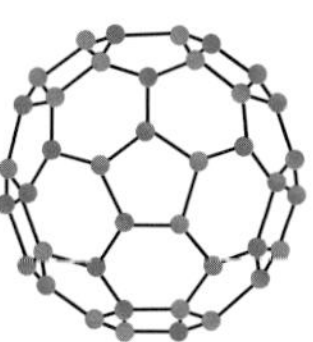

Fullerene (C_{60})

LET'S BE CLEAR ABOUT GLASS

Glass can be pretty SHATTERING! For one thing, its closest cousin is something that you can't see through, won't cut you, and gets inside your bathing suit.

TINKLE!

The best place to make glass is at the beach or in the desert. WHY? Because its main component is silicon dioxide (also known as silica), which most commonly occurs as sand! The silica is mixed with sodium carbonate to reduce its melting point and with lime (calcium oxide) to harden it into glass.

Don't try melting sand from the beach to get glass. You'd have to heat it to about 3,632°F (2,000°C)!

Adding oxides

Many types of glass can be made by adding metal oxides to the silica. Oxides are compounds that contain the oxide ion (an oxygen species with a negative charge). The most common type of glass is soda-lime glass. It has a silica base with sodium and calcium oxides added. It's cheap, tough, and easy to recycle.

Need a reminder? Check out ions on pages 12-13.

Really COOL Science Bit

Is glass a LIQUID or SOLID?

This is something that chemists love to argue about. It's complicated—VERY complicated! You might hear people claim that glass is a liquid. It's true that glass is a bit CRAZY, but it's NOT a liquid. Instead, glass is an amphorous solid: its atoms are not arranged in as regular a pattern as most solids. That gives it some properties similar to liquids (but it's still NOT a liquid!). Try "pouring" some glass—it's not happening! If you had a glass that was full of, umm…glass, and you wanted to "pour" the glass out of the, er…glass, it might happen…but you'd have to wait billions of years! That's no liquid!

CRACK!

WHAT'S IT MADE OF?

silicon, oxygen, sodium, calcium, lead, and boron; with copper, cadmium, cobalt, gold, nickel, and tin added for color

Fancy glass

Expensive glassware (sometimes called "cut" glass or "crystal") used in making chandeliers and fine glassware is basically soda-lime glass with the calcium oxide replaced with lead oxide. This glass is highly polished and reflects and refracts light to "sparkle."

Glass for the oven, glass for test-tubes

Adding boron oxides to the basic soda-lime glass mixture produces "borosilicate" glass. This glass is very resistant to heat and temperature changes, so it can be used for ovenware and laboratory glassware. This type of glass is often better known by its trademarked name "Pyrex."

TRY THIS

Make SUGAR GLASS

Have you ever seen someone thrown through a pane of glass in the movies? Spectacular, isn't it? But it's also pretty dangerous with real glass. That's why they use this sugar glass instead.

What you'll need

baking sheet
non-stick spray
2 cups (500 mL) water
3 1/2 cups (875 mL) sugar
1 cup (240 mL) corn syrup
1/4 cup (50 mL) cream of tartar
an old saucepan
a kitchen thermometer

1. Use the non-stick spray to coat the baking sheet.
2. Place the water, sugar, corn syrup, and cream of tartar in the saucepan and heat the mixture until it starts to boil.
3. Let the mixture boil, stirring constantly, until it reaches 300°F (150°C).
4. Pour the mixture onto the greased baking tray.
5. Allow the mixture to cool and harden and then use a knife to loosen the sheet of sugar glass and pop it out carefully from the edge.

Make sure you read THIS: Sugar glass is hygroscopic, which means that it attracts water, so it will soften soon after being made. You have to use it really quickly, or it's more like rubber than glass!

DISH THE DIRT ON SOAP

WHAT'S IT MADE OF?

carbon, hydrogen, potassium OR sodium, oxygen

How does soap KNOW what's dirt and what isn't? You might not believe it, but it all comes down to electrical charge. Let's come clean about soap.

Soaps are usually the sodium or potassium salts of fatty acids. Sodium and potassium are often interchangeable since they have similar properties. That's why they're in the same group of the periodic table: group 1—the Alkali Metals. A fatty acid is an organic compound made up of a long chain of carbon atoms that contains a carboxylic acid functional group, COOH. In soap, the hydrogen in the carboxylic acid group is replaced by a sodium ion (Na^+) or potassium ion (K^+) to form a "salt." The sodium and potassium ions make one end of the soap molecule polar, which means it has an electrical charge; the charge means it can dissolve in polar (charged) water—LIKE DISSOLVES LIKE!

Carboxylic acids contain carbon, oxygen, and hydrogen.

A functional group is a bunch of atoms that control how an organic molecule behaves.

SLIP!

Really COOL Science Bit

Ho-hum, you've got scum!

Scum is a sign of soap gone bad. If your soap won't produce a lather—and doesn't really clean things—you're probably suffering from hard water. Hard water contains ions of calcium (Ca^{2+}) and magnesium (Mg^{2+}). These ions are from group 2 of the periodic table: the Alkaline Earth Metals. Unlike group 1 ions, they form INSOLUBLE compounds with the fatty acids in soap…which leads to the formation of scum.

ELEPHANT TOOTHPASTE

If you've tried to clean an elephant's teeth, you know that you need a LOT of foamy toothpaste. Here's how to make some for the next time. Please ask the elephant before cleaning its teeth.

WHAT YOU'LL NEED

3% (or better still, 6%) hydrogen peroxide
dried baker's yeast
dishwashing liquid
food coloring
...and lots of space!

1. Find a tall, thin empty bottle (glass or plastic).
2. Place about 1/2 cup (125 mL) of hydrogen peroxide into the bottle along with a squirt of dishwashing liquid and some food coloring.
3. Mix the yeast packet with a small amount of warm water, leave it for a couple of minutes, and then add it to the bottle.
4. Stand back!
(Make sure that you have plenty of newspaper on the floor, or better still do this experiment outside or in the bath!)

How does that work?: The yeast acts as a catalyst to release the oxygen gas tied up in the hydrogen peroxide. The gas rushes out, bringing the dishwashing liquid bubbles and food coloring with it. You may also notice that the mixture gets very HOT. That's because the chemical reaction is exothermic, meaning that it generates heat.

Coming clean

A soap molecule has two distinct parts: a hydrophilic (water-loving) part and a hydrophobic (water-hating) part. The hydrophilic ends of the soap molecules mean that they can be dissolved and used in water. The hydrophobic ends of the soap molecules get away from the water by finding any dirt, oil, and grease and attaching themselves to it. Then they "lift" the nasty things from whatever you are cleaning.

POP!

Burning Questions about GASOLINE

Without gasoline, the planet would come to a standstill. It's so useful that countries have fought WARS to control supplies of the oil it's made from. When gasoline burns, its vapors drive engines.

What a gas!

Organic molecules are sometimes "cracked" to produce smaller molecules that combust better.

Gasoline is a mixture of hydrocarbons (organic molecules made from carbon and hydrogen). Carbon atoms can form chains and rings with one another, and gasoline consists of molecules that have between 4 and 12 carbon atoms joined together. Hydrogen atoms hang off the carbon chains and rings to complete the molecules. Gasoline is one of the many products made from crude oil. Others are diesel, jet fuel, paraffin wax, tar, asphalt, and lubricants. They're all hydrocarbons. Crude oil forms in the ground over millions of years from living matter that has been heated and pressurized.

SQUIRT!

WHAT'S IT MADE OF?

carbon, hydrogen, oxygen, but NOT lead (not any more, anyway!)

WHOOOSH!

Internal COMBUSTION

Gasoline is combustible. That means it can mix with oxygen, ignite, and burn. When a hydrocarbon mixture burns, it produces not only a lot of heat but also carbon dioxide and water vapor gases. It's these hot gases that make gasoline so useful. They expand and apply a force to the pistons in an engine, which then cause the wheels of the vehicle to turn. The chemical reaction for combustion looks like this:

$$C_xH_y + (x + y/4)O_2 \rightarrow xCO_2 + (y/2)H_2O$$

(x and y are the number of carbon atoms and hydrogen atoms in the hydrocarbon, respectively).

This makes your car go!

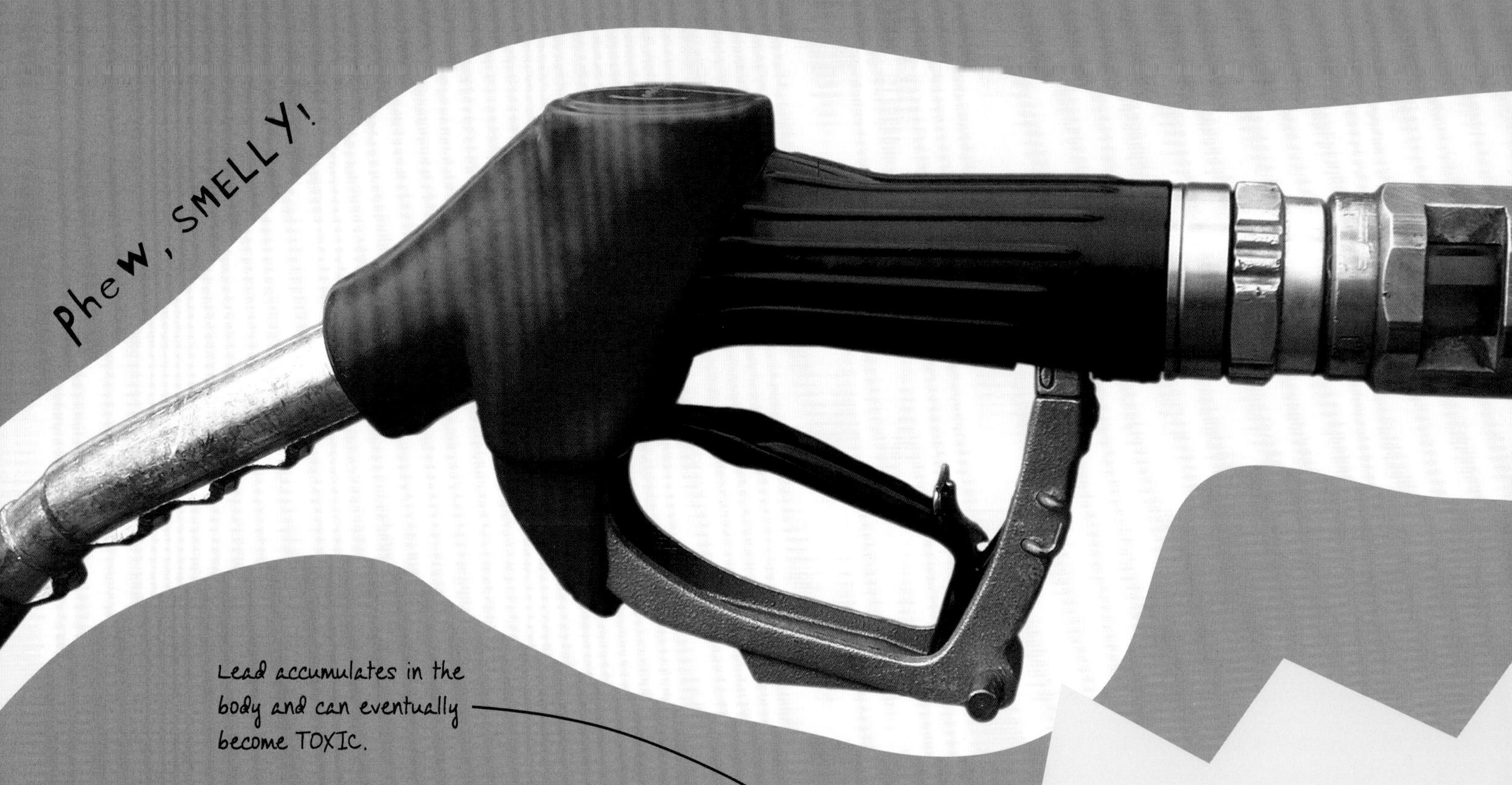

Lead accumulates in the body and can eventually become TOXIC.

What's that knocking?

Sometimes gasoline can ignite and burn at the wrong time in an internal combustion engine. When it does, it causes "knocking," and the engine becomes much less efficient. Starting in the 1920s, lots of lead compounds were added to gasoline to reduce the effects of knocking and make the engine more efficient. This "leaded" gasoline was phased out in the last quarter of the 20th century when it was discovered that lead compounds had damaging effects upon both the environment and people! Now most gasoline is "unleaded."

Important safety tip

Gasoline is made from crude oil. So is TAR. But don't try filling your parents' car with bits of tar from the road. It will clog the engine! Also, gasoline is highly flammable. So don't light FIRES near gas pumps. (You probably guessed that already, right?)

Going GREEN

Like all natural resources, crude oil will run out one day. Alternative fuels are becoming more and more popular. Cars are now being made that run on hydrogen, electricity, ethanol (an alcohol), and bio-fuels (made from vegetable oil). That reflects accelerating concerns over the environmental impact of burning hydrocarbons, such as the "Greenhouse Effect" (caused by rising levels of carbon dioxide from combustion). Some alternative fuels produce much less pollution. For example, when hydrogen burns it only produces water! $2H_2 + O_2 \rightarrow 2H_2O$.

THE POWER OF ATTRACTION

Have you ever felt irresistibly drawn toward something? (No, not a candy store!) Magnetism is one of the most mysterious forces on Earth.

What's a magnet? Well, a magnet is any material that creates a magnetic field! Not much help? A magnetic field is an area that creates a force that can act on ferromagnetic materials. That is still a bit misleading. "Ferro" means "iron" BUT not all ferromagnetic materials contain iron! They are usually made from a combination of three elements: iron, cobalt, or nickel. But elements like manganese, copper, oxygen, and some rare earth elements can be included, too. Magnets usually attract or repel other ferromagnetic materials depending on how their poles line up.

"Rare earth elements" is a name used for the Lanthanoid elements plus scandium and yttrium.

Poles are the opposite ends of a magnet, known as north and south. Opposite poles attract.

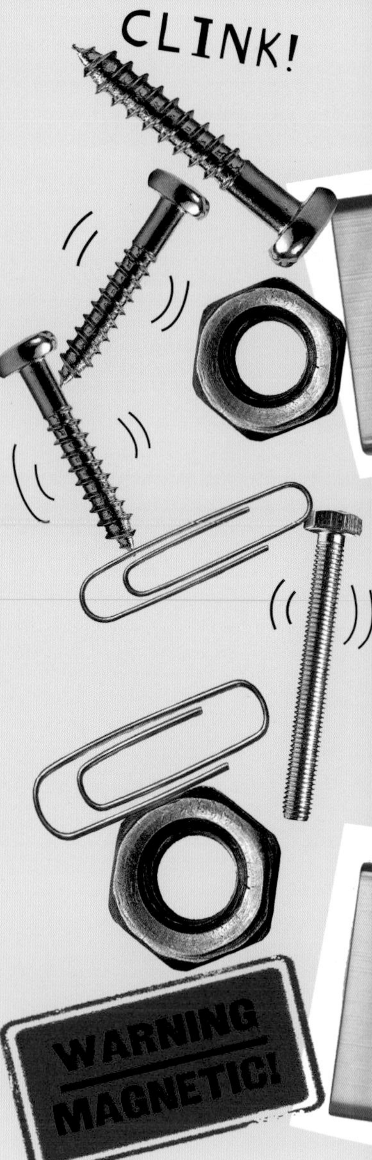

How does magnetism work?

It depends on one of the subatomic particles inside an atom. The electron is the negatively charged particle found around the nucleus of all atoms. In some materials, these electrons are not paired with a mate; they naturally create a small magnetic field of their own. Since even the smallest magnet has trillions of atoms, when the electrons all line up in one direction we get a much larger magnetic field. Hey presto, a magnet!

WHAT'S IT MADE OF?

iron, cobalt, nickel, and a few others

Hard and soft

A magnet with a permanent magnetic field is sometimes called "hard." Some ferromagnetic materials can be magnetized when placed in the field of a hard magnet, but they lose their magentism once they have been removed; they are called "soft" magnets.

Make an ELECTROMAGNET

Electrical current = magnetism: what could be simpler?

WHAT YOU'LL NEED

a "D" battery
a few yards of thin copper wire
a 6-in. (15-cm) iron nail
some metal paper clips

1. Attach one end of the copper wire to one terminal on the battery.
2. Carefully coil the copper wire around and around and around the length of the iron nail, making a long coil along the whole length of the nail but leaving some of the nail sticking out of the end of the copper coil.
3. Attach the other end of the wire to the other terminal in the battery.
4. Bring the end of the iron nail close to some paper clips. What happens?

How does that work?: When electrons flow in a wire, they create a small magnetic field. Usually you don't experience the magnetic field very much because it is so weak. Coiling the copper wire around the nail creates lots of tiny magnetic fields that add up to one BIG one.

N

S

Earth's magnetic field

There is a huge amount of iron in the core of the Earth. It's the fourth most abundant element in the Earth's crust behind oxygen, silicon, and aluminum. The result is that Earth has its own magnetic field. This is REALLY useful if you want to find your way around. A compass is pretty handy if you are lost!

A compass—which is just a tiny magnet—always lines up with the Earth's magnetic field: it will point due north.

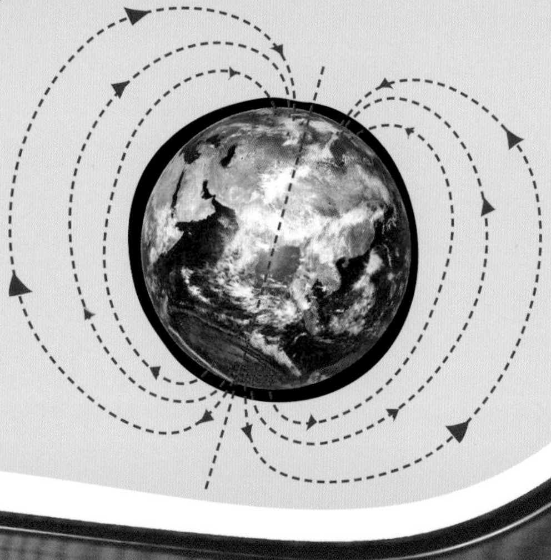

SKYSCRAPERS

If you've ever dropped a brick on your foot, you won't be surprised to learn that stone buildings are quite heavy. That makes it difficult to build them really, really tall.

The only way our ancient ancestors knew to build tall structures was by making the bottom of the buildings large enough to support the massive weight of all of the stones. The pyramids of ancient Egypt are an example. The base of the structures—their footprint —became increasingly large as pharaohs built themselves taller and taller pyramids. Of course, this used more and more land. That might not be much of a problem in the Egyptian desert, but imagine how impractical—not to mention expensive—it would be in the growing American cities of the late 19th century.

Bessemer "steels" the show!

Pig iron is formed when iron ore is treated to extract the iron. It contains about 4 percent carbon, which makes it brittle and useless for construction.

In the second half of the 19th century, Englishman Henry Bessemer patented a process that allowed pig iron to be converted into STEEL. In the Bessemer process, oxygen is blasted through the pig iron to remove impurities, and the amount of carbon drops to less than 2 percent. The resultant alloy is really tough and strong. It allowed engineers to design buildings using a skeleton of large steel beams. The walls no longer had to carry any weight, so they didn't have to be heavy stone. That made the whole building lighter, so it did not need a huge footprint. Buildings could now go UPWARD rather than spreading OUTWARD, and so the skyscraper was born.

WHAT'S IT MADE OF?

carbon, iron

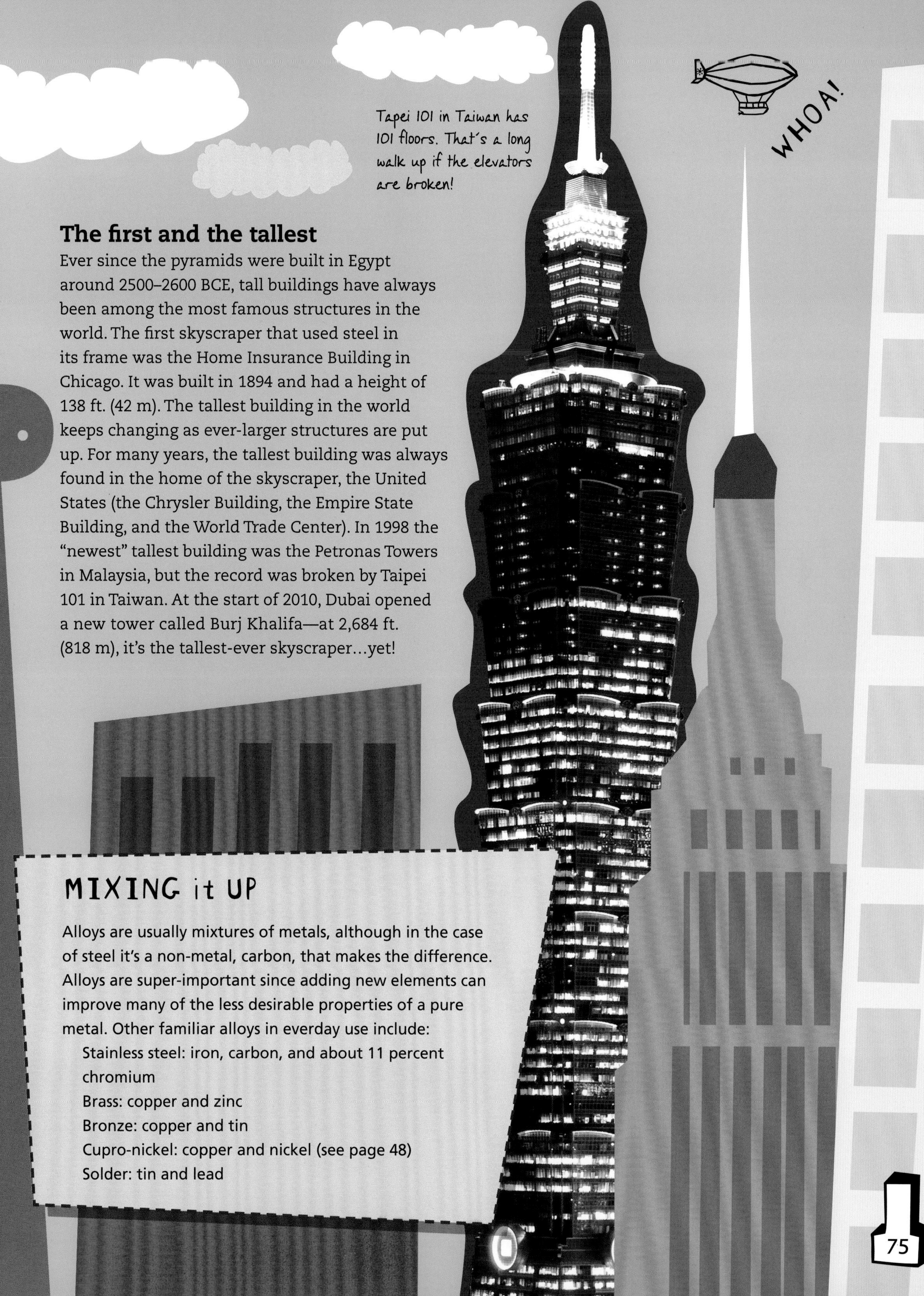

Tapei 101 in Taiwan has 101 floors. That's a long walk up if the elevators are broken!
WHOA!

The first and the tallest

Ever since the pyramids were built in Egypt around 2500–2600 BCE, tall buildings have always been among the most famous structures in the world. The first skyscraper that used steel in its frame was the Home Insurance Building in Chicago. It was built in 1894 and had a height of 138 ft. (42 m). The tallest building in the world keeps changing as ever-larger structures are put up. For many years, the tallest building was always found in the home of the skyscraper, the United States (the Chrysler Building, the Empire State Building, and the World Trade Center). In 1998 the "newest" tallest building was the Petronas Towers in Malaysia, but the record was broken by Taipei 101 in Taiwan. At the start of 2010, Dubai opened a new tower called Burj Khalifa—at 2,684 ft. (818 m), it's the tallest-ever skyscraper...yet!

MIXING it UP

Alloys are usually mixtures of metals, although in the case of steel it's a non-metal, carbon, that makes the difference. Alloys are super-important since adding new elements can improve many of the less desirable properties of a pure metal. Other familiar alloys in everday use include:

Stainless steel: iron, carbon, and about 11 percent chromium
Brass: copper and zinc
Bronze: copper and tin
Cupro-nickel: copper and nickel (see page 48)
Solder: tin and lead

Ra
Landing gear down
Si
What's on TV?
H
F
Db
Kr
WARNING FAST CAR!
Can I DRIVE?
U
Ho

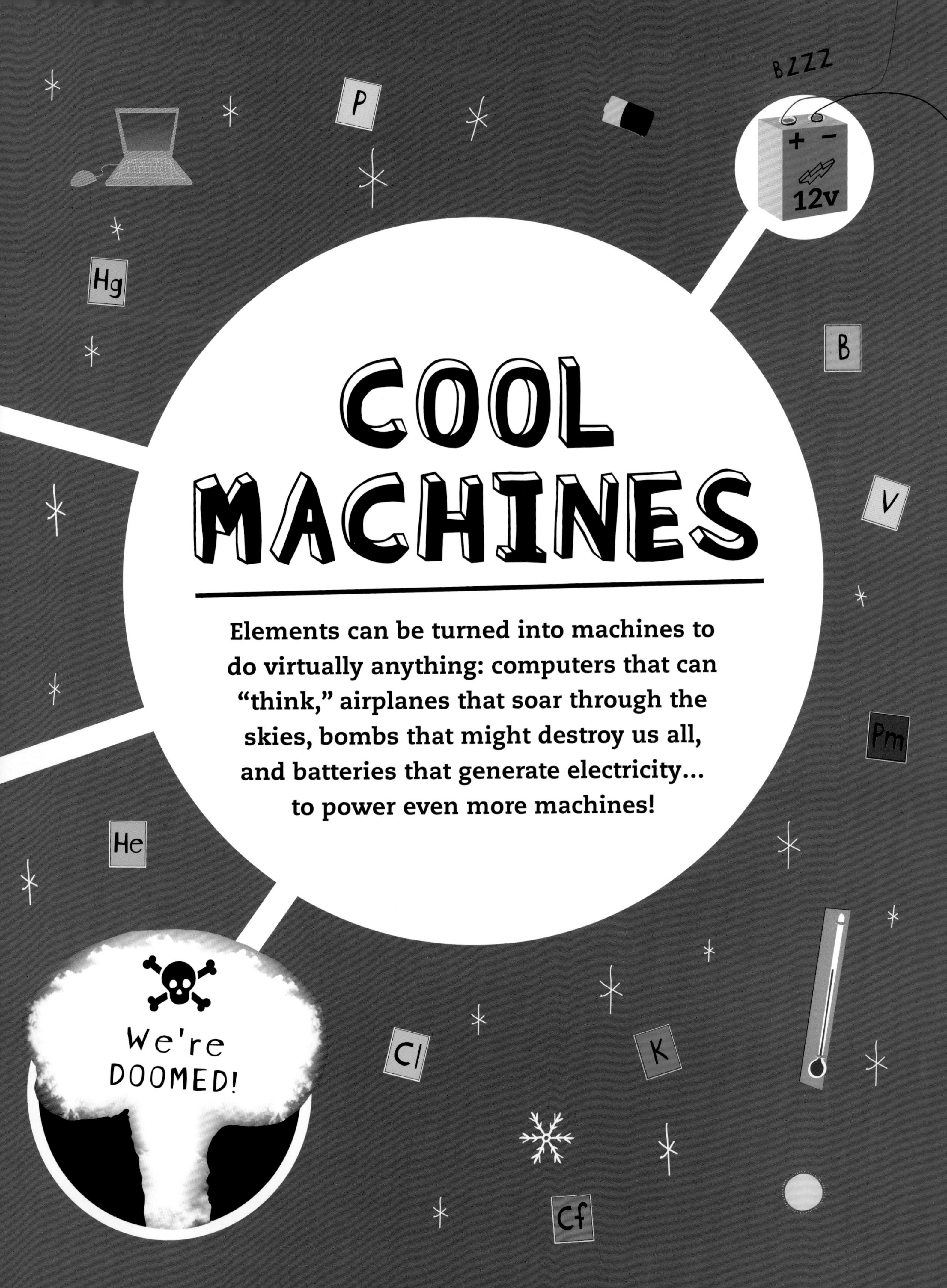

COOL MACHINES

Elements can be turned into machines to do virtually anything: computers that can "think," airplanes that soar through the skies, bombs that might destroy us all, and batteries that generate electricity... to power even more machines!

WHAT'S IT
MADE OF?
silicon, boron,
phosphorus,
gallium,
arsenic

Count on Your COMPUTER

At the heart of all computers is a "silicon chip." But not the salt and vinegar kind! The term describes a small electronic microprocessor that works by altering the properties of silicon.

When metals conduct, they use "free" electrons to carry electrical current. Silicon has four such electrons, but silicon atoms form a lattice that ties them all up in chemical bonds. That makes silicon a poor conductor, but other elements can change things.

A lattice is a bunch of particles arranged in a regular, organized pattern like a cube.

Don't be a dope!

Silicon, with its four bonding electrons, is found in group 14 of the periodic table. Elements in groups 13 and 15 have three and five bonding electrons respectively, so they can change the conductivity of the silicon.

Elementary stuff

Silicon

- **Atomic Number: 14**
- Atomic Mass: 28.09
- **Isotopes: 3**
- Boiling Point: 5,252°F (2,900°C)
- **Melting Point: 2,577°F (1,410°C)**

Silicon is the second most abundant element in Earth's crust, where it occurs in rocks and minerals such as quartz. It's versatile, so it turns up everywhere: in the silicon chip that revolutionized modern life; in glass and products such as sealants, rubbers, and resins; and in the silica gel packets used to keep electronics dry. Quartz is used in watches for precision timing, and silicon gel is used to treat burns.

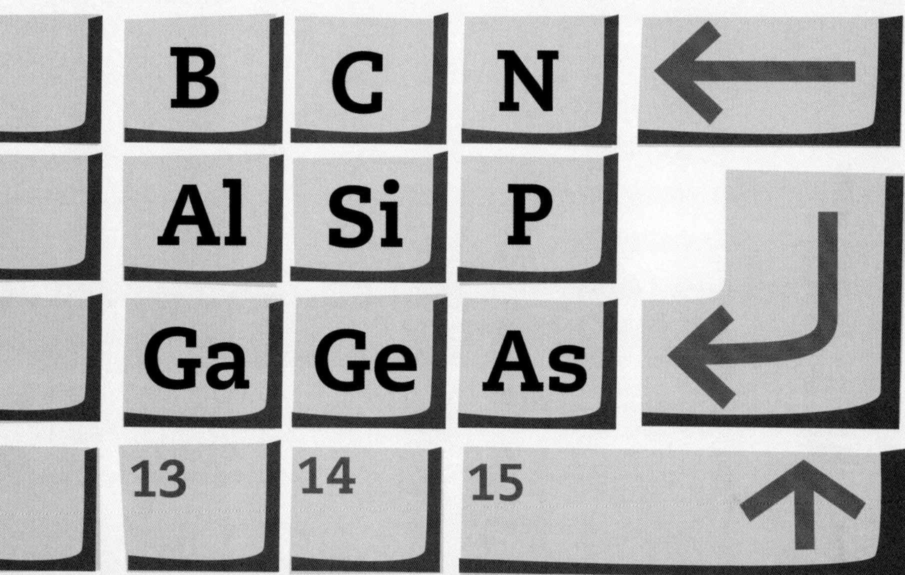

Groups 13 and 15 are the keys!

With a tiny amount of phosphorus or arsenic (group 15), which both have an extra electron compared to silicon, silicon becomes a good conductor. The extra electrons carry the electric current.

These are called N-type semiconductors, because the extra electrons carry a negative charge.

Gallium or boron from group 13 can also improve silicon's conductivity. With only three electrons, they introduce "holes" to the silicon. The silicon electrons tend to jump from one hole to another, which allows the electrical current to flow. This type of semiconductor is called a P-type since the absence of (negative) electrons makes the semi-conductor relatively positive. The process of introducing these other elements is called "doping."

Places where electrons should be but aren't.

CHILL OUT!

BRRR!

Food and drinks are the only interesting things in your fridge, right? Wrong! What about the hidden gases that make a fridge really cool?

Why is it important?

The fridge is one of the most important modern appliances. All food contains bacteria that can cause it to go bad: chilling food slows that process. Before modern refrigeration was invented, food was usually preserved by either salting or pickling. Refrigeration is far more convenient.

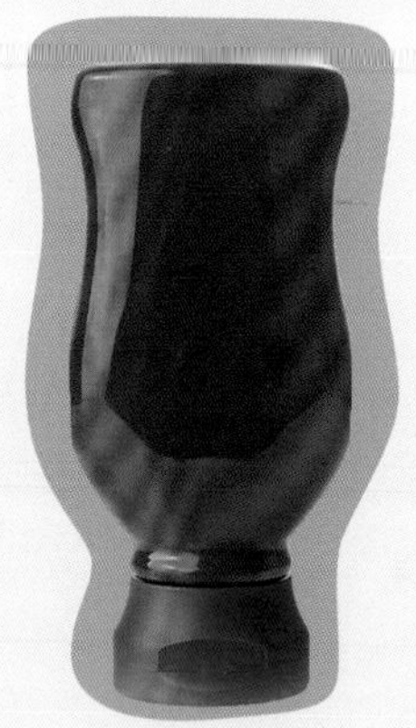

Don't ADD cold—TAKE heat

A liquid refrigerant is pumped through a compression valve into a refrigerator, where it rapidly expands and becomes REALLY COLD. The super-cold gas passes through coils inside the fridge. The heat from the contents of the fridge is absorbed by the gas, leaving the food compartment cold. The refrigerant gas starts to warm up, so it is pumped out of the fridge via a compressor (which makes it even hotter) to coils outside the cooling compartment at the back or bottom of the fridge. The hot coils give out heat to the room, and the gas cools and turns back into a liquid. The liquid is then pumped back into the fridge, and the cycle repeats.

WHAT'S IT MADE OF?

carbon, fluorine, hydrogen (but no longer chlorine)

What about freezers?

A freezer has more coils inside than a fridge, and the food compartment inside is often smaller. This means it can cool down a little more, and the temperature drops below freezing.

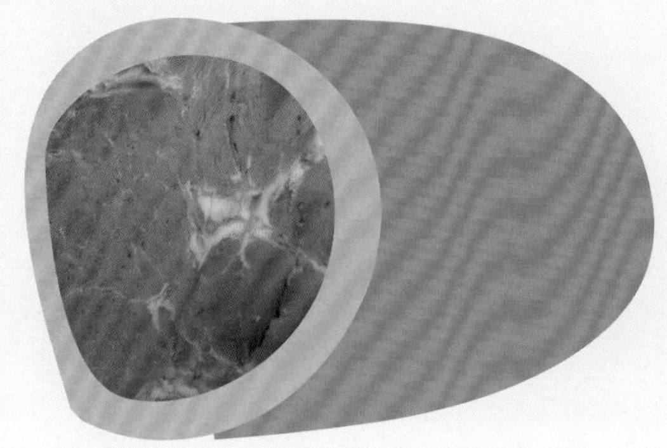

TRY THIS

Make ICE CREAM

A quick and easy way to make a frozen treat, but it has some great chemistry in it.

WHAT YOU'LL NEED

1 cup (250 mL) cream
1 cup (250 mL) milk
1 tsp. (5 mL) vanilla
5 tbsp. (75 g) sugar
resealable food bags
1 egg
crushed ice
rock salt

1. Make a batch of ice-cream mixture by mixing the cream, milk, and sugar in a resealable food bag with the egg and vanilla. Place about a quarter of the mixture into another food bag. Carefully push the air out from the bag and seal it tightly.
2. Fill a third food bag with crushed ice.
3. Add several handfuls of rock salt to the ice.
4. Place the sealed ice-cream mixture bag inside the ice bag and seal the outer bag.
5. Gently squeeze the mixture for about 20 minutes or until the ice cream forms!

HOW DOES THAT WORK?: Adding salt to the ice causes the freezing point of the H_2O to fall below its normal freezing point, 32°F (0°C). This is known as "Freezing Point Depression." It's called a colligative property, and it depends on the amount of substance present—more salt means a lower freezing point. Eventually the bag will get cold enough to freeze the ice-cream mixture and make it solid. This is why we put salt on the roads in winter, so that the weather will have to reach really low temperatures before the salty water will freeze.

Elementary stuff

Fluorine

- **Atomic Number: 9**
- Atomic Mass: 18.99
- **Isotopes: 1 naturally occurring isotope**
- Boiling Point: –306˚F (–188˚C)
- **Melting Point: –363˚F (–220˚C)**

Fluorine is the most reactive element: it forms bonds with just about anything. This halogen is a yellowish gas that is often added to water or toothpaste to help strengthen teeth. Fluorine is also present in well-known organic compounds like CFCs (chlorofluorocarbons). CFCs were once used in fridges, but they damaged the ozone layer by converting ozone (O_3) to oxygen (O_2) and were mostly banned. Another place you'll find fluorine is in the non-stick polymer known by the trade name "Teflon."

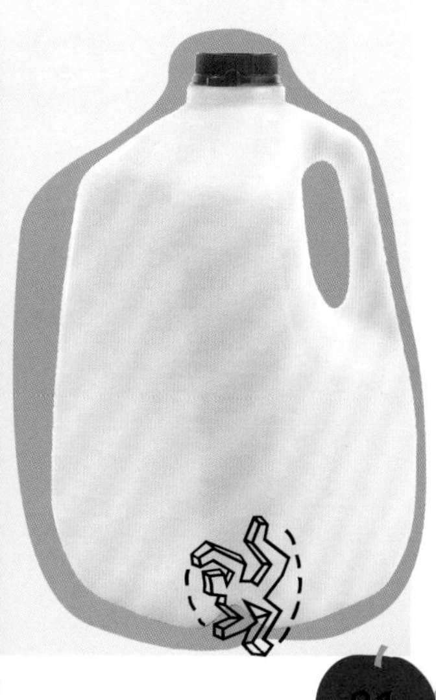

BOOM, BOOM, SHAKE THE ROOM

Although nuclear reactions take place on a tiny scale, they release vast amounts of energy: enough to fuel a power station...or make an atomic bomb. There are two sorts of reactions: fission and fusion.

Gone fission?

Nuclear power relies on reactions between the nuclei (that's the plural of nucleus) of atoms. The nucleus is the dense center of the atom that contains protons and neutrons, but not electrons. The process of "splitting" an atom's nucleus apart is called "fission." Fission releases energy, which can be used to heat water that drives turbines and creates electricity.

Each atom that splits only releases a small amount of energy, but a very small piece of uranium contains billions of atoms, and together the nuclear reactions can create a large amount of energy.

WHAT'S IT MADE OF?

uranium, hydrogen

Uranium-235 is the isotope of uranium that splits and sustains a nuclear chain reaction. Uranium-238, which is more common, won't work!

$E = mc^2$

You may have seen Albert Einstein's famous equation, $E = mc^2$. What does it mean? Well, it simply predicts that when a nuclear reaction takes place, some of the mass (m) of the nuclei will be converted to energy (E).

Chain reactions

Uranium-235 atoms can be split by firing a neutron at them. When the neutron hits the nucleus, it splits it into smaller pieces and the energy is released. When an atom of Uranium-235 splits, some of the products are more neutrons. These neutrons can crash into other U-235 atoms, and the process is repeated. That produces even more neutrons, and a chain reaction can take place. This can rapidly get out of control and can be very dangerous. It was a fission reaction, for example, that powered the atomic bombs dropped on Hiroshima and Nagasaki in Japan in 1945, at the end of the Second World War.

Be Careful!

Nuclear power can be dangerous! There were bad accidents at Chernobyl in Ukraine in 1986 and at Fukushima in Japan in 2011. Nuclear accidents kill people and release radioactive material that makes people sick. So if you're going to build a nuclear reactor, get some ADULT supervision.

Confused about fusion?

Nuclear fusion is the opposite of fission. In fusion, atoms are brought together to form heavier particles. This process also produces large amounts of energy. One of the common uses of fusion is in the hydrogen bomb, where hydrogen nuclei are brought together.

BRAIN BOX

ERNEST RUTHERFORD

From Down Under to the center of things (1871–1937)

From "Down Under" (New Zealand to be precise), Rutherford was passionate about radioactivity. In fact, he won the 1908 Nobel Prize in Chemistry for his investigations into the disintegration of the elements and the chemistry of radioactive substances. But Rutherford's most important work came a couple of years later, when he did a famous experiment firing alpha particles at a sheet of gold foil and predicted the existence of a nucleus at the center of all atoms.

LET'S FLY!

The first airplanes were made of wood, canvas, and even paper. That's not such a good idea for huge jets. They need a material that's very light but still VERY strong.

You can call me Al

The frames of most modern aircraft have usually been made of aluminum and its alloys. Up to 75 percent of a modern aircraft's weight can be put down to element number 13. Aluminum is a great metal for the job because it is light and it resists corrosion (rusting). There's one problem, though: pure aluminum isn't actually especially STRONG...which could present a problem at 35,000 feet! Usually aluminum is alloyed with lots of other elements to make it stronger, as in duralumin, where it is mixed with copper, magnesium, and manganese.

Don't throw out your old jumbos

Since it takes a lot of electricity to produce aluminum, it is not a cheap metal to make. So reusing aluminum is very important. If you have any old, aluminum soda cans, make sure that you recycle them—and the

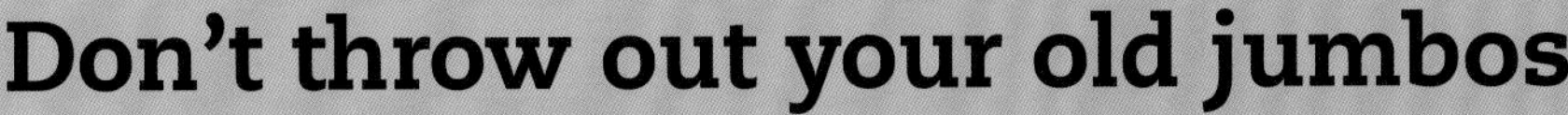

Aluminum

- **Atomic Number: 13**
- Atomic Mass: 27.00
- **Isotopes: 1 naturally occurring isotope**
- Boiling Point: 4,566˚F (2,519˚C)
- **Melting Point: 1,220˚F (661˚C)**

Aluminum is the third most common element in Earth's crust (behind silicon and oxygen), but it's not easy to get at. Aluminum is so hard to extract that it was once more valuable than silver or gold. In the 1880s a process was developed that used electricity to turn aluminum ore (commonly called bauxite, Al_2O_3) into the pure metal. Suddenly aluminum was a lot LESS precious and a lot MORE common.

WHAT'S IT MADE OF?

aluminum, titanium, carbon, hydrogen, and many other metals for alloying

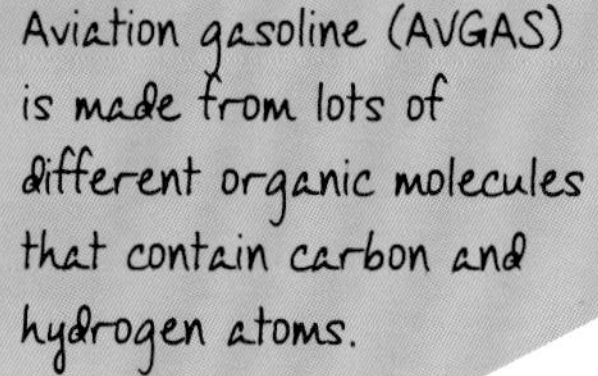

Aviation gasoline (AVGAS) is made from lots of different organic molecules that contain carbon and hydrogen atoms.

same goes for any old 747s that you might have lying around the house. (Hint: look under the stairs or in the attic!)

Metal fatigue

Some of the very latest aircraft, such as the Boeing 787 Dreamliner, are replacing large amounts of aluminum with a new material called Carbon Fiber Reinforced Polymer (CFRP for short). This material has carbon fibers woven together with organic polymers made of carbon, hydrogen, and oxygen. CFRPs are even lighter than aluminum and are even more resistant to corrosion.

Anagram alloys

Another metal used extensively in aircraft manufacture is element number 22, titanium. As well as sounding a bit like aluminum, it is also very light. Unlike aluminum, it is very strong in its pure form and it is especially resistant to heat. That makes it great for use in aircraft engines. Again like Al, Ti is often used as an alloy, and some of these metal mixtures have CRAZY names like Ti–6Al–4V and Ti–6Al–2Sn–4Zr–2Mo! You can probably guess that these names come from the percentages of other elements, like tin (Sn), zirconium (Zr), aluminum (Al), vanadium (V), and molybdenum (Mo), which are mixed with the titanium (Ti) in the alloys.

PEDAL TO THE METAL

READY
STEADY
GO!

To hit speeds of over 215 mph (350 km/h), Formula 1 cars have to be light and aerodynamic, but strong enough to survive the G-forces and heat generated by accelerating and braking.

Carbon fiber is nearly a perfect answer. It is very strong, very light, and changes very little when heated. It has one drawback—it costs a fortune. Carbon fiber is made by turning carbon atoms into long fibers that are twisted together like yarn. Other carbon-based materials like PICA (known as "phenolic carbons") were originally developed for heat shields to protect spacecraft from huge temperatures when they re-entered Earth's atmosphere. In a racing car, they are used for brakes and any other components that get very hot during the race.

Race-car designers joke that the perfect material would be an imaginary element called "unobtanium." (UNobtainable!)

Normal car tires are inflated with air, but that wouldn't work in racing car tires, which get extremely hot when racing. The water vapor in normal air can easily be heated. That changes the tire pressure, and the car will not handle so well. Most racing tires are inflated with nitrogen-rich gases or carbon dioxide, both of which change less as they get really hot. The tires themselves are complicated mixtures of rubber-like polymer hydrocarbons (compounds of carbon and hydrogen).

FUELS

It might be a surprise, but the fuel that powers a modern racing car is not that different from the regular gasoline you put in an ordinary car.

TRY THIS

Spool RACING CAR

Not exactly Formula 1, but fun to do and it's about TEN BILLION dollars less expensive!

WHAT YOU'LL NEED

- a candle
- an empty spool of thread
- a match
- an elastic band
- a pencil

1. Cut a length from the candle, remove the wick, and create a small hole through the middle.
2. Thread the elastic band through the center of the candle piece and the middle of the spool.
3. Break the match in half and pass it through the elastic band to secure it on the opposite side of the spool from the candle.
4. Pass the pencil through the elastic band at the candle end.
5. Wind the pencil around and around until the elastic band is really tight.
6. Put the racer down and let it rip!

How does that work?: The candle is made from paraffin wax, a hydrocarbon with between 20 and 40 carbon atoms and lots of hydrogen atoms. It acts as a good lubricant. Potential energy gets stored in the elastic band when it is wound up by the pencil. As the rubber band unwinds, it releases this potential energy, which is converted to kinetic energy (movement)!

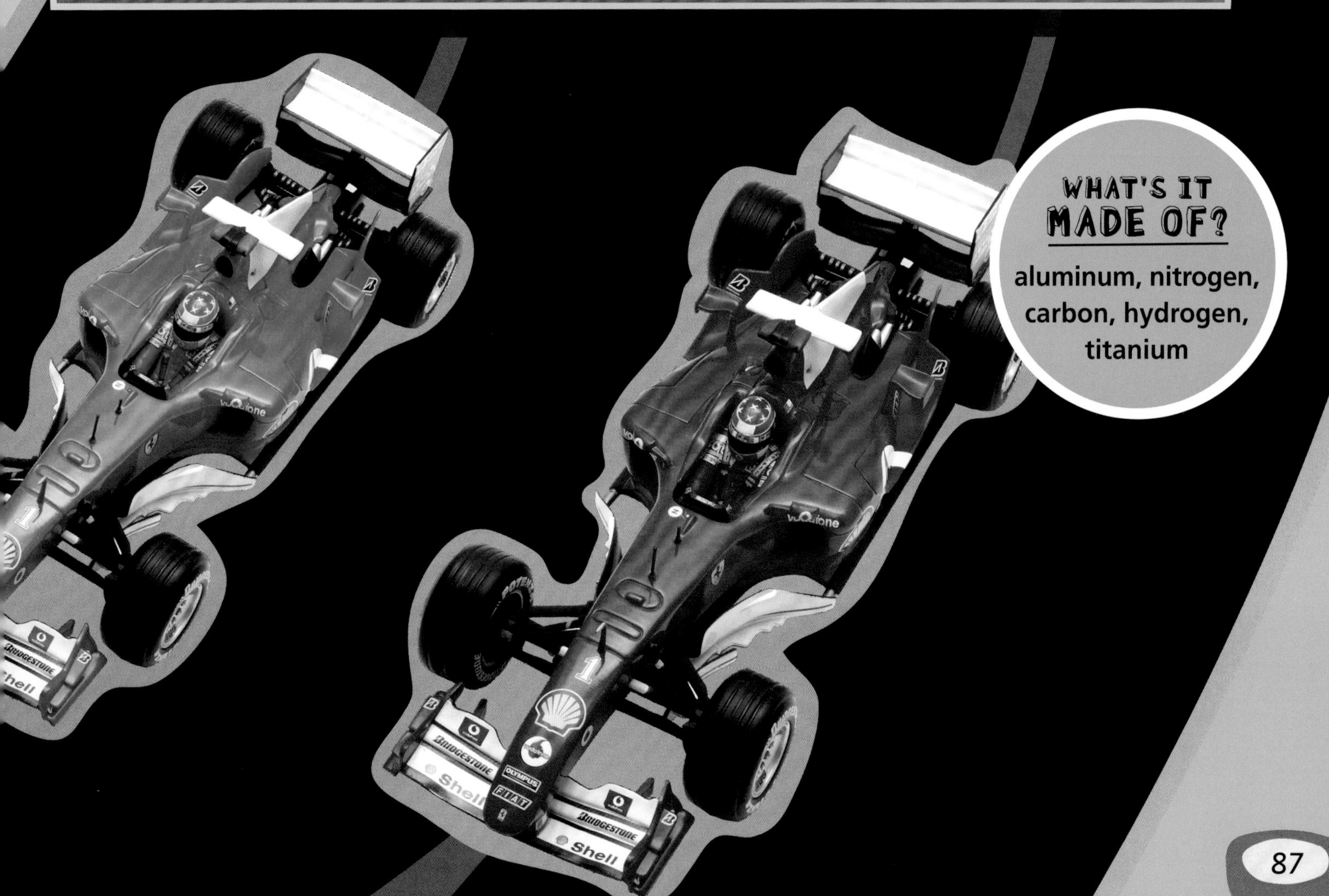

WHAT'S IT MADE OF?

aluminum, nitrogen, carbon, hydrogen, titanium

READY, SET, CHARGE!

A power station can be a bit heavy to carry around. Luckily, a battery can produce the same result—electricity—and it's a lot more portable.

Electron SHIFT!

Take a look at any kind of battery and you will see two terminals: one marked positive (+) and one marked negative (-). Inside the battery, a bunch of electrons gather on the negative terminal. If you connect a wire between the negative terminal and the positive terminal, the negatively charged electrons will charge (charge!—get it?!) around to the positive one. The flow of electrons is called "electricity," and if you put an electrical device somewhere on the wire (like an iPod), then the electricity can be put to use to "POWER" the device.

Remember, in charged particles, opposites attract.

CLANG!

BZZ!

Chemistry goes ELECTRO

How do we get electrons to move around inside a battery? All batteries contain two chemical substances. One would really like to LOSE electrons; placed opposite it is another that would really like to GAIN electrons. The substances are connected using an electrolyte (a liquid or paste that can conduct). When you connect the two terminals, the electrons flow around from negative to positive—ELECTRICITY! When either the chemical that is losing the electrons has given them all away, or the chemical that is accepting electrons cannot take any more, the battery is "dead." The process of losing electrons is called oxidation, and the gaining of electrons is called reduction. Together we call the process REDOX. Redox reactions are the basis of all electrochemical reactions used in batteries to produce electricity.

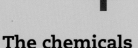

WHAT'S IT MADE OF?

zinc, lead, nickel, magnesium, cadmium, oxygen, potassium, lithium, carbon, hydrogen, sulfur

Recharging—BACKWARD!

Some materials that are used in batteries can have the electrons sent BACK (from positive terminal to negative terminal) so the process can happen all over again. That means the battery is rechargeable. Once the battery is recharged, the electrons are sent around the circuit again (from negative to positive), creating more electricity...until it's time for the recharging process again.

The chemicals

What type of chemicals can be used in batteries? Well, there are many, many possibilities, some involving pure elements, others involving compounds. Metals are common, since they usually want to lose electrons. The most common combo used in the simplest batteries is a zinc and carbon mixture. Here are some other common combinations that you may have heard of:

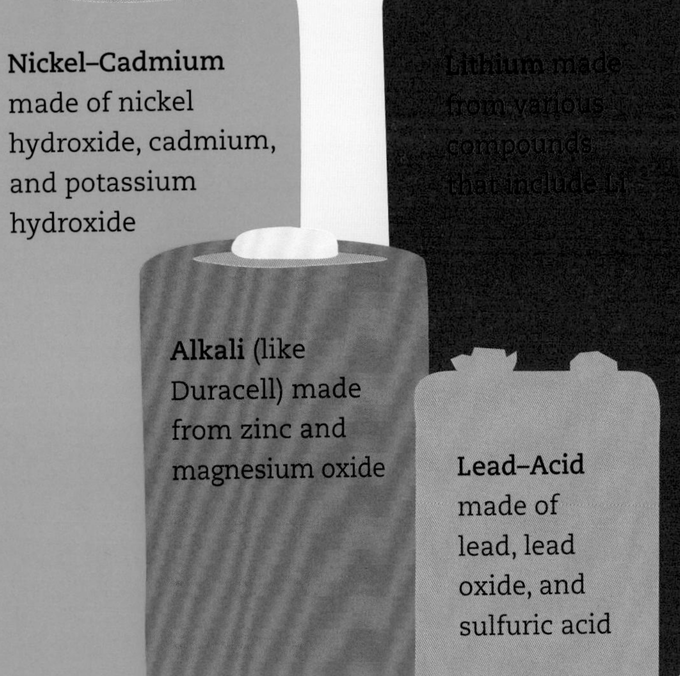

Nickel–Cadmium made of nickel hydroxide, cadmium, and potassium hydroxide

Lithium made from various compounds that include Li

Alkali (like Duracell) made from zinc and magnesium oxide

Lead–Acid made of lead, lead oxide, and sulfuric acid

Different batteries have different applications. Considerations such as cost, size, and longevity (how long they last before they "die") influence which type is used where.

WHAT'S ON TELEVISION?

The cool thing about TV isn't just what's on the box—it's what's inside the box. It might not come as a surprise that the TV set is actually very, very complicated.

Taking the tube

A television works thanks to lots of complicated physics, but the chemistry relies on something called phosphorescence. Phosphorescence is the process of light emission that occurs when radiation (energy) strikes a chemical material known as a phosphor. The cathode ray tube (CRT) in a television fires a beam of electrons at a screen that is coated with a phosphor which, depending on its chemical make-up, will emit light of a certain color that persists for different lengths of time.

Physics is the study of how matter and energy interact.

Phantastic phosphors

The phosphors in TVs are VERY complex and often contain transition metals or rare earth metals from the central part of the periodic table. Common ones used in phosphors include zinc (Zn), silver (Ag), iron (Fe), cobalt (Co), copper (Cu), europium (Eu), cerium (Ce), terbium (Tb), and manganese (Mn).

WARNING
DON'T BE A COUCH POTATO!

BRAIN BOX

A SCIENTIFIC TAG TEAM

(Marie Curie 1867–1934; Pierre Curie 1859–1906)
The Curies were an extraordinary family of French–Polish scientists. Between Marie, her French husband Pierre, their daughter Irene, and their son-in-law Frederic, the Curies won no fewer than FIVE Nobel Prizes! Marie was the first person ever to win two Nobels, and she went on to discover two new elements: polonium (named after her native Poland) and radium. She mainly investigated radioactivity, in which she pioneered the use of radioactive isotopes in medicine. In the end, radiation sickness was probably what killed her.

These elements are included in complicated compounds with other elements such as aluminum (Al), oxygen (O), sulfur (S), silicon (Si), indium (In), gallium (Ga), and chlorine (Cl). Luckily, you don't have to remember all those ingredients to watch your favorite show—you can just press a button!

WHAT'S IT MADE OF?

rare earth elements, transition elements, and a selection of zinc, silver, iron, cobalt, aluminum, sulfur, silicon, indium, silver, cobalt, europium, manganese, oxygen, cerium, chlorine, terbium, or gallium

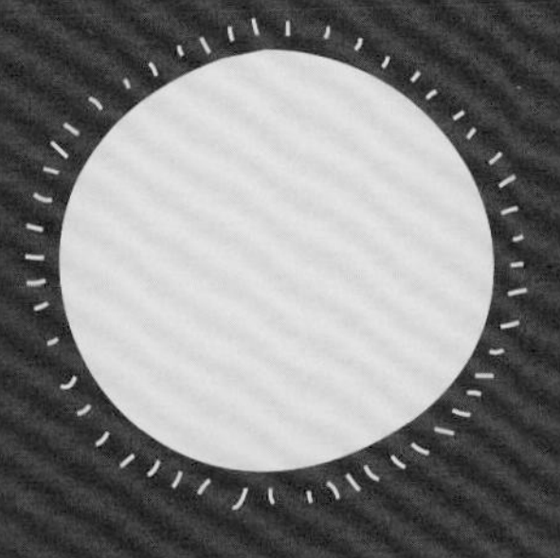

Taking the Temperature

Heat changes the properties of chemicals. That's why it's possible to measure temperatures. (And why you know whether you're HOT or COLD.)

The heat is on

Thermometers were made as early as the 11th century.

All thermometers work on the same principle. If the particles in a liquid are heated, they gain energy and expand. If the liquid is held in a sealed glass tube, it will rise or fall in the tube according to the temperature of the surroundings. The hotter the surroundings, the more the liquid will expand and the further up the glass tube it rises. "Thermo" is the Greek word for warm and "meter" is the Greek word for measure.

What's inside?

Some of the earliest thermometers used water. They had one obvious problem. Once the temperature fell to 32°F (0°C),

Elementary stuff

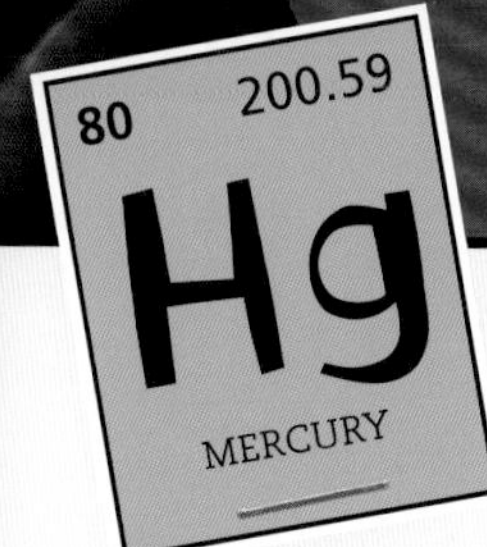

- **Atomic Number: 80**
- Atomic Mass: 200.59
- **Isotopes: 7 natural isotopes**
- Boiling Point: 674˚F (357˚C)
- **Melting Point: –38˚F (–39˚C)**

Mercury

Mercury, once called "quicksilver," is one crazy element (and the only metal that is a liquid at room temperature). Alchemists thought mercury was present in all metals and could help turn base metals into gold. It is toxic, especially its vapors—mercury nitrate used to drive hat makers who used it mad. Mercury was used in thermometers and barometers, but in many countries it is now banned.

WHAT'S IT **MADE OF?**

carbon, hydrogen, oxygen, silicon (for the glass), mercury (but not anymore—poisonous!)

40

0

-40

0, 32, or 273? It's the SAME!

The usual ways to record temperature are Fahrenheit, Celsius, and Kelvin. In 1742, Daniel Fahrenheit came up with the scale named after him. It gave the freezing point of water a value of 32°F and its boiling point 212°F. Anders Celsius produced a similar scale, but he separated water's freezing and boiling by 100 degrees. (His scale is sometimes called centigrade, as "centi" means 100.) Lord Kelvin's scale gave the value ZERO to the coldest possible temperature (which he calculated was –273°C). It was later found to be more precisely –273.15°C or ABSOLUTE ZERO. The coldest temperature ever recorded naturally on Earth is about 128.2°F (–89°C)!

the water froze, making them useless to measure very cold temperatures. The most common liquids today are either mercury (the silver, liquid metal) or alcohol with a dye added (these are the thermometers with a red or blue liquid inside). Modern thermometers usually use the colored alcohol mixture since mercury has many health hazards associated with it and has been banned in many countries.

Really COOL Science Bit

Converting temperatures

It is fairly simple to convert from one temperature to another. The table below shows how to convert any temperature to another on a different scale.

From	to °F	to °C	to °K
Farenheit		Minus 32, then multiply by 5/9	Minus 32, then multiply by 5/9, then add 273.15
Celsius	Multiply by 9/5, then add 32		Add 273.15
Kelvin	Minus 273.15, then multiply by 9/5, then add 32	Minus 273.15	

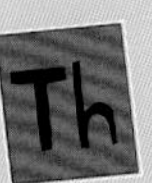

COOL WORDS

anions Ions that have a negative charge.

atom The smallest part of an element that retains the properties of the element. Atoms have a nucleus that contains protons and neutrons, and electrons that are found outside the nucleus.

atomic number The number of protons in an atom.

catalyst A substance that speeds up a chemical reaction.

cations Ions that have a positive charge.

chemical change A process during which new substances are formed.

chemical equation A shorthand way to summarize a chemical change.

chemical formula A shorthand way to show the number and type of each particle in a substance.

combustion A substance's reaction with oxygen, better known as "burning."

compound Two or more different atoms joined together chemically in fixed quantities.

covalent bonds A shared pair of electrons.

density Mass per unit of volume.

electron The sub-atomic particle with a negative charge.

element A substance that consists of only one type of atom.

endothermic Describes a process that absorbs heat from the surroundings.

exothermic Describes a process that gives off heat to the surroundings.

half-life The amount of time it takes for half the nuclei of a radioactive material to decay.

inert Resistant to reaction.

ion A charged particle created by atoms either gaining or losing electrons.

isotopes Atoms of one element with the same number of protons and electrons but different numbers of neutrons.

mass number The sum total of protons and neutrons in the nucleus of an atom.

mixture A random combination of two or more substances that are not chemically bonded to one another.

molecule A small group of atoms chemically bonded.

neutron The sub-atomic particle with no electric charge (neutral).

nucleus The dense center of an atom that contains the protons and neutrons.

physical change A process during which substances only change state and no new substances are formed.

physical property A property that can be measured without considering the chemistry of a substance.

products The substances that are formed when a reaction is complete.

proton The sub-atomic particle with a positive charge.

radioactive decay A natural process during which the nucleus of an element spontaneously changes, which often produces a new element and is accompanied by the emission of other particles and energy.

reactants Substances initially present in a chemical reaction.

salts Ionic compounds formed when the hydrogen ions of an acid are replaced with another positive ion.

solute The substance dissolved in a solution.

solution Mixture of a solute and a solvent.

solvent The liquid part of a solution in which something is dissolved.

states of matter Solid, liquid, or gas.

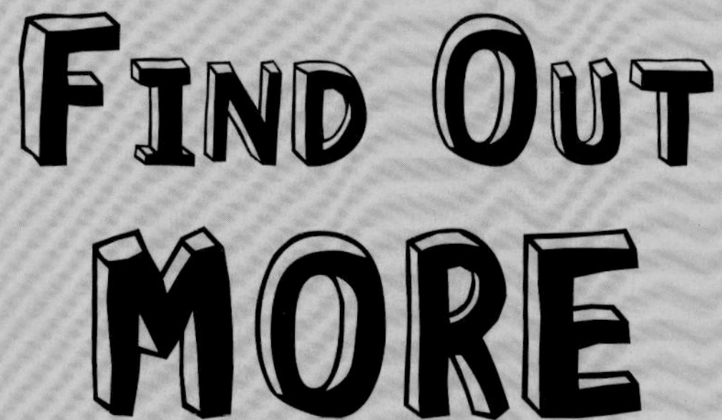

BOOKS

Atkins, Peter W. *The Periodic Kingdom: A Journey Into the Land of the Chemical Elements*. New York: Basic Books, 1997.

Dingle, Adrian, and Simon Basher (illus). *The Periodic Table: Elements with Style*. London: Kingfisher, 2007.

Emsley, John. *Nature's Building Blocks: An A–Z Guide to the Elements*. Oxford: Oxford University Press, 2003.

Emsley, John. *Molecules at an Exhibition: Portraits of Intriguing Materials in Everyday Life*. Oxford: Oxford Paperbacks, 1999.

Stwertka, Albert. *A Guide to the Elements*. Oxford: Oxford University Press, 2002.

Gray, Theodore. *The Elements: A Visual Exploration of Every Known Atom in the Universe*. London: Black Dog and Leventhal Publishers Inc, 2009.

Scerri, Eric R. *The Periodic Table: Its Story and Its Significance*. Oxford: Oxford University Press, 2006.

WEBSITES

http://www.rsc.org/chemsoc/visualelements/PAGES/pertable_fla.htm
A visual periodic table from the Royal Society of Chemistry: click on any element to see its profile.

http://www.periodic.lanl.gov
An informative site for students, published by the Los Alamos National Laboratory.

http://www.ptable.com/
Dynamic periodic table showing elements' properties, electronic configuration (orbitals), and isotopes.

http://www.adriandingleschemistrypages.com/
My own site, full of chemistry information for students and teachers—and don't forget to check out my blog!

INDEX

CREDITS

Page 4 (top left), 6–7: Patrice Loiez, Cern/Science Photo Library
Page 37 (bottom right): Chris O'Reilly/Nature Picture Library

All other photographs Shutterstock; All interior artworks BRG; Cover artworks Clive Goddard.